ENGLISH
COSTUME

PORTRAIT OF THOMAS EGERTON, VISCOUNT BRACKLEY, LORD HIGH
CHANCELLOR 1596-1617

ENGLISH COSTUME
FROM PREHISTORIC TIMES TO THE
END OF THE EIGHTEENTH CENTURY

BY

GEORGE CLINCH
F.S.A. Scot., F.G.S.

WITH ONE HUNDRED AND THIRTY-ONE ILLUSTRATIONS

EP Publishing Limited
Rowman & Littlefield
1975

First published in 1909 by Methuen & Co.

This edition published 1975 by
EP Publishing Limited
East Ardsley, Wakefield
West Yorkshire, England

and in the United States of America by
Rowman & Littlefield
Totowa, New Jersey

ISBN 0 7158 1070 7
(EP Publishing)

ISBN 0 87471 617 9
(Rowman & Littlefield)

Please address all enquiries to EP Publishing Limited
(address as above)

Printed in Great Britain by
REDWOOD BURN LIMITED
Trowbridge & Esher

CONTENTS

v

TO

THE RIGHT HONOURABLE

HAROLD ARTHUR

VISCOUNT DILLON, V.P.S.A.

ONE OF THE FOREMOST AUTHORITIES ON

COSTUME AND ARMOUR

THIS LITTLE BOOK IS BY SPECIAL PERMISSION

INSCRIBED BY THE

AUTHOR

PREFACE

THE scope of the present work, as indicated by the title given to it, may seem sufficiently comprehensive. Possibly it may appear too ambitious, but it is obviously impossible, in a volume of this size, to treat the subject of English Costume in full detail, and it would be almost as difficult to confine it to any particular section or sections of the subject which would be agreeable to all readers.

The writer has therefore attempted to take a middle course, and has endeavoured to cover the whole of the ground by dealing with the main facts, without professing to be exhaustive. Pictorial illustrations have been freely used as being more convenient and intelligible than verbal descriptions. When possible these have been drawn from first-hand and contemporary sources. Illuminated MSS., sepulchral effigies, monumental brasses, paintings, statuary, ancient wills, inventories, and the contents of the chief museums, are the authorities upon which the author has mainly relied for his materials; but he has also gratefully made use of much of what has already been written in the works of Messrs. Fairholt, Planché, J. G. Waller, H. Druitt, and Viscount Dillon. In his attempts to get at the actual facts of this interesting subject, he has drawn from every available source, and, he trusts, with due acknowledgment; and he is also indebted to Viscount Dillon for much special and valuable information, for the loan of books from Ditchley, and for the loan of the woodblock printed on page 203; to Mr. Mill Stephenson, F.S.A., for much valuable help and for the loan of most of the woodcuts printed in the text; to Mr. Justice Phillimore and Mr. Arthur Denman, F.S.A., for assistance in describing legal costume; for some useful hints and suggestions to Mr. W. H. St. John Hope (from whose published papers some of the information in the following pages is derived); to Mr. Emery Walker, F.S.A., for permission to use the photographs from the paintings illustrating scenes in the life of St. Etheldreda; to the Society of Antiquaries of London for permission to reproduce photographs from the paintings of St. Etheldreda, photographs from the coloured illustrations of the Louttrell Psalter, and numerous engravings on Archæologia; to the authorities of the Victoria and Albert Museum, South Kensington, particularly Mr. Arthur B. Skinner, F.S.A., for most courteous assistance; and to Dr. G. F. Warner, F.S.A., keeper of the Department of MSS. in the British Museum, for special facilities in connection with the examination of manuscripts in his department illustrative of English costume.

SUTTON, SURREY
31st March, 1909

ILLUSTRATIONS IN TEXT

xi

LIST OF PLATES

xv

LIST OF PLATES xvii

INTRODUCTION

THE study of costume, it has long been generally acknowledged, is one of most fascinating interest, not alone to ladies, in whose domain primarily it may be supposed to lie, but also to the student of history, the sculptor, the painter, and indeed everyone who desires to look behind the dry pages of written history for evidences of the actual everyday life of the people.

The present work is the result, within limited space and imperfect as the author is only too conscious, of an attempt to realize the various changes of fashion and developments of thought of the people of England during past ages in phases which are shown far more accurately and intimately by the vanities and follies of costume and fashion than by the sober matter-of-fact writings of the old chroniclers.

It cannot be doubted that the whole subject of costume is of great interest to a very large number of people, and no civilized individual can be wholly indifferent to it. The forms and fashions in which dress has at different times been worn are, it will be generally admitted, at once an index to the tastes, the fancies, and the vanities of their wearers.

In this attempt to trace the evolution of English costume, advantage has been freely taken of what is already recorded on the subject; but many other sources of information, some of them new it is believed, have been drawn upon. These include not only the obvious sources, such as sculpture, statuary, and monumental effigies, both in the round and in the form of monumental brasses, but also those incidental sidelights afforded by testamentary documents, inventories, paintings, illuminated manuscripts, pictures, portraits, and also the actual clothes themselves which have escaped the ravages of the insidious moth, the destructive influences of wear, and the even more disastrous, because more thorough, ordeal of spring-cleaning.

The main purpose of the book is to explain and illustrate the ordinary, everyday clothes of the people during the past centuries, the garments for special and official purposes being given a subsidiary place in the volume.

The sources of information on the subject of English costume are by no means of uniform character nor of equal value.

Monumental brasses, from the ease with which they may be mechanically copied by heel-ball rubbings, have long been recognized as a valuable source of information, and this they unquestionably are, but there are many things about costume which they do not show.

Sepulchral effigies in the round are of far greater value as evidence for costume than monumental brasses, because of the clearness with which different garments may be traced out, a task far from easy in flat plates of engraved brass.

But, valuable as effigies are, they form a by no means invariable guide to the actual costumes ordinarily worn by the persons represented. It will constantly be found that in their sepulchral effigies certain persons are shown in official or formal costume rather than their everyday common garb. Thus, priests and bishops are shown in eucharistic or processional vestments, and sovereigns sometimes in their coronation robes, and usually with the royal crown on the head; but we must not infer from this that these were the vestments and robes worn in ordinary, everyday life.

The use of such garments in carving the effigies of the dead was simply a convenient method of showing symbolically the rank or profession of the wearer. As a matter of fact, the sovereign of the Middle Ages wore his crown only upon very rare and special occasions, and mass-vestments were specially and exclusively worn at the celebration of mass in the church. Bishops did not walk about the streets wearing the mitre and carrying their episcopal staff, as one might infer from representations given on the modern theatrical stage; neither was a complete suit of cumbersome armour the regular walking attire of

the knight, as some of the popular novelists would
have us believe.

In order to understand the motives and forces
which shaped ancient costume it is essential to remember that mediæval people were common-sense
men and women. Comfort, convenience, and pro-
priety were the chief principles which influenced
them in the choice of materials and shapes for their
clothing. It is not exaggeration to say that nothing
has done more to obscure and confuse popular ideas
on ancient costume than the gorgeous and over-
elaborated representations of great historical dramas
which have been furnished by our theatrical authorities during the past twenty or thirty years. The
defects may not be in bad taste, indeed many are
certainly very attractive, but they are due in the first
place to a misconception and misreading of the evidence on the subject, and secondly to a very natural
desire to produce striking spectacular effects.

ENGLISH COSTUME

ENGLISH COSTUME

CHAPTER I

PREHISTORIC COSTUME

THE form and fabric of the clothes first worn by human beings are questions which we can hardly expect to fully settle with the evidence now available. Owing to their very nature and purpose, garments would generally be worn into shreds before they were finally abandoned, and actual remains of the earliest of them, therefore, must necessarily be of extreme rarity if they exist at all.

By a happy circumstance, however, it happens that we are not left in entire darkness as to the kind of clothing which was worn by prehistoric man. The palæolithic cave-dwellers of France have left many remains, the most remarkable of which are unquestionably the spirited sketches scratched on bones, etc., and generally representing animals of various kinds. The extraordinary skill displayed in these sketches, showing the animals of the period with life-like fidelity, has long been one of the wonders of prehistoric archæology. Within the last few years further sketches were obtained by the late Monsieur

Piette from the cave deposits at Brassempouy, Mas-d'Azil, etc., among which are some which picture human beings. Some of these figures are represented partially nude, or wearing tight-fitting leg-coverings, but in others it is quite easy to distinguish the garments represented. One very remarkable torso of a small human figure found at Brassempouy is specially noteworthy. It is not a sketch, but a carving in the round in ivory. The body garment, or tunic, which is quite plain, reaches barely to the thigh, where it terminates abruptly in a straight horizontal edge. The legs, a large part of which remains, are either quite nude or covered by garments which fit quite closely. On another fragment of carved ivory a human head is represented showing that the hair, which is parted apparently on both right and left sides and round the back of the head, descends to the lower part of the neck behind, and is cut off straight a little above the eyebrows in front. The whole of the hair appears to be arranged in separate locks, being either plaited or tied round at frequent intervals to prevent the inconvenience of tangling.

In the Cavern of Gourdan a bone was found upon which is a sketch of seven individuals walking in single file. The sketch is hardly definite enough to show whether any clothing is worn, or whether the head and shoulders are partly covered by long hair falling from the head. The legs are either nude or covered with trouser-like garments. The figures are apparently intended to represent women.

Another representation of the upper part of a woman,

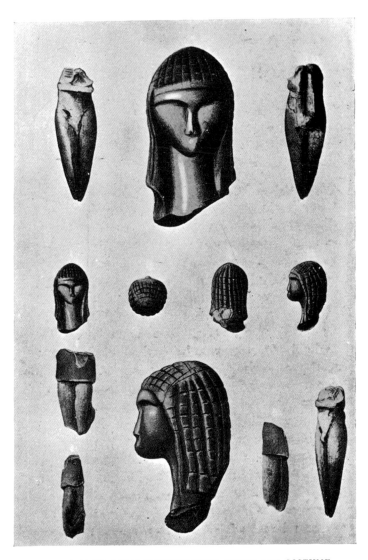

CARVINGS IN BONE REPRESENTING STONE AGE COSTUME

carved out of part of a tooth, was found at Mas-d'Azil. The only garment shown seems to be a collar round the neck, unless the natural furrows in the tooth are intended to indicate the folds of a gown.

In the Neolithic Age we have no representations of the human figure which enable us to found any opinion as to the costume worn. The remains of spindle-whorls and other indications of spinning and weaving found on Neolithic sites show with sufficient clearness that articles of clothing were not confined to the skins of animals, but that some kind of cloth material was manufactured.

Professor Boyd Dawkins[1] gives the following useful summary of the subject :—

The arts of spinning and the manufacture of linen were introduced into Europe in the Neolithic Age, and they have been preserved with but little variation from that period down to the present day in certain remote parts of Europe, and have only been superseded in modern times by the complicated machines so familiar to us. In the Neolithic household the spindle and the distaff were always to be found, and the circular perforated spindle-whorls, made sometimes of stone, and at other times of pottery or bone, are very commonly met with in the Neolithic habitations and tombs. The thread is proved, by the discoveries in the Swiss lakes, to have been composed of flax, and the combs, which have been used for pushing the threads of the warp on to the weft, show that it was woven into linen on some kind of loom. It is very probable also that the art of making woollen cloth was also known, although from its perishable nature no trace of it has been handed down to us.

[1] *Early Man in Britain*, p. 275.

The Neolithic Age was succeeded by the Bronze Age, a period, or stage, of human culture extending from the introduction of bronze to the introduction of iron. Of this period we have more certain knowledge, the contents of numerous sepulchral mounds, or barrows, explored in England having enabled us to form a fairly complete idea of the costume, dress, arts, and pursuits of the Bronze Age folk.

The following particulars as to the clothing and personal ornaments in use during the Bronze Age in Britain are mainly taken from the lucid account given by Professor Boyd Dawkins,[1] who has collected his facts from various eminent authorities on prehistoric archæology, including Sir A. W. Franks, Canon Greenwell, Keller, Montelius, etc.

The rich and the chiefs were clothed in linen or in woollen homespun. In Scandinavia they wore woollen cloaks, and a round woollen cap on the head, and their legs and feet were protected by leather leggings and sandals. A dagger, attached to the girdle in a sheath of wood or leather, and an axe were their constant companions. The face was shaven, and the beard, moustaches, or whiskers were sometimes plucked out. The hair was worn long, and arranged into a pyramid sufficiently large, in some cases, to allow of the use of a hairpin twenty inches long. Ear-rings, necklaces, and pendants and amulets of stone, bone, glass, bronze, and even gold were also worn. Bracelets made flat, round, or hollow, and

---

[1] *Early Man in Britain*, pp. 355–8.

BRONZE AGE COSTUME

ornamented with various designs, usually of chevron form, adorned the wrists.

Both spinning and weaving were arts known to the Bronze Age people, as they were also to those of the Neolithic Age. Spindle-whorls, loom-weights, and bone weaving-combs have been found in considerable numbers both in the Bronze Age and in the Early Iron Age. They furnish the most incontestable proof that spinning and weaving were arts quite well known to our prehistoric ancestors. Of the actual fabrics spun and woven into cloth, however, but very few specimens remain.

One of the most important pieces of Bronze Age clothing in this country was found buried in a rough oak coffin in a barrow at Scale House, near Rylston, in the West Riding of Yorkshire. Canon Greenwell, who personally directed the work of excavating the sepulchral mound or barrow, gives the following particulars :— [1]

The coffin was formed of the trunk of an oak tree split in two and then hollowed out. It was $7\frac{1}{4}$ feet long and 1 foot 11 inches wide. The hollow within was 6 feet 4 inches long and 1 foot wide, roughly hewn out, and still showing the marks of the tool employed ; the ends inside were finished off square. It was not possible to make out the precise nature of the tool which had been employed, but the appearances warranted the conclusion that it had been a narrow-edged metal implement.

[1] *British Barrows*, pp. 375-6.

The body had gone to decay. It had been enveloped in a woollen fabric, enough of which remained to show that it had reached from head to foot. It was very rotten, and it was impossible to recover any but small parts of it, or to prove whether the body had been laid in the grave in its ordinary dress or simply wrapped in a shroud. It is on the whole probable that in this case, as in those of some tree-burials discovered in Denmark, the person had been interred in the dress worn by him in daily life, though, perhaps, it may be alleged that the absence of anything like a button or other fastening is rather against that view. The material is now of a dark brown colour, due most likely to the tannin in the oak of the coffin.

Canon Greenwell adds that he sees no reason for hesitating to refer this interment to the people whose usual custom it was to place the body of the dead person in a stone cist or in a grave within the barrow ; merely supposing that in this and in a few other instances they departed from their ordinary practice in favour of a wooden receptacle.

Several other Bronze Age burials in Britain have been found resembling this just described as far as the rude coffin or receptacle for the dead is concerned, but in no case have remains of clothing been found. In the tree-coffins of Denmark, also of the Bronze Age, the clothes worn by the deceased during life have been found interred with the body.

From a certain Bronze Age grave in Jutland some very remarkable articles of woollen clothing were procured some years ago by Messrs. Warsaae and Herbst.

These comprised a cloak, skirt, shawls, caps, and leg-gings, all made of woollen stuff. Traces also were found of leather articles, probably boots, at one end of the wooden coffin in which the body had been interred. Amongst other things found were sword, brooch, knife, double-pointed awl, a pair of tweezers, and a large double button, or stud, all of bronze; a small double button of tin, and a javelin-head of flint.

The Bronze Age was followed by the period usually called the Early Iron Age, extending up to the begin-ning of the Roman occupation of Britain. During this age, although there is abundant evidence as to the metallic ornaments, weapons, etc., there is not much definite information on the question of costume. That spinning and weaving were carried on is made quite clear by the numerous spindle-whorls, loom-weights, and weaving-combs found in association with remains characteristic of the time.

The inhabitants of Britain during the Early Iron Period were the race usually known as Ancient Britons. The Druids, who combined the duties of instructing youth and celebrating religious rites, have been often figured and described in historical works, but the information we possess as to their costume and general appearance is of an indefinite and unreliable character, and largely built up on the conjectures of seventeenth and eighteenth century antiquaries, consequently, it must not be accepted without caution. However, as we shall presently show, some evidence of the Druids has been found in France.

That the Ancient Britons used a variety of dyed
materials for their clothing is pretty certain. Blue,
obtained from woad, is believed to have been the
favourite colour, and this may have given rise to the
tradition which credits them with dyeing the body
by way of ornament. It is certain that in such a
climate as that of Britain warm clothing must have
been necessary for a great part of the year, and every-
thing points to the probability that fogs and rain
were more prevalent at the time of the Ancient
Britons than they are at the present day.

From the writings of Julius Cæsar we learn that
the inhabitants of the interior of Britain wore
clothing made of the skins of animals ; but, whilst
the internal parts of the country were in a very
barbarous and elementary condition as far as garments were concerned, it is certain that those who
dwelt near the coasts (particularly the coasts of the
south-eastern parts of Britain), and enjoyed the
advantages of intercourse with occasional visitors
from the Continent, were much better provided for
in the matter of personal attire, woven stuffs being
worn instead of the skins of animals.

The civil dress of those Britons who were seen by
Julius Cæsar when he effected a landing on our
shores was probably identical with that of the Gauls,
who we know, from Roman statues in the Louvre
and other sources, were usually clothed in three
garments, viz.—

(i) Braccæ, or trousers, an article of dress by
which the barbaric nations generally seem to have

been distinguished from the Romans. They were made by the Gauls and Britons of their striped or chequered cloth, called breach, brycan, or breacan, breac in Celtic signifying anything speckled, spotted, striped, or in any way parti-coloured.

(ii) Over the braccæ, or breeches, as we now call the garment, was worn a body-garment with short sleeves, and reaching a little below the knees. This was called the tunic.

(iii) The cloak, or mantle, called sagum, from the Celtic word saic (which, according to Varro, signified a skin or hide, such having been, as we have seen, the material which the invention of cloth had superseded), was, in Britain, of one uniform colour, generally either blue or black, while the predominating tint in the chequered tunic and trousers was red.

The general character of the costume of the ancient Gauls and Britons still survives in a measure in the dress of the Scottish Highlanders. This was probably the usual habit of every Celtic tribe at the time of the appearance of the Roman legions on our shores, and it is a matter of no small interest to find traces of the costume still existing among us.

There remains yet another article of dress to be mentioned which adds another connecting link between the ancient Britons of the past and the modern Gaelic inhabitants of our islands. We refer to the shoes of untanned leather, made of raw cow-hide with the hair turned outwards—identical, in fact, with the brogues of Ireland and the Scottish Highlands.

The chin was shaved by men of rank amongst the

Gauls and Britons, but immense tangled moustaches
were worn, so much so that Strabo describes those of
the inhabitants of Cornwall and the Scilly Isles as
hanging down upon their breasts like wings. The
hair was turned back over the crown of the head, and
fell down in long and bushy curls behind.

The ornaments of the Britons consisted, like those
of the Gauls, of armlets, bracelets, and rings of gold,
silver, brass or copper, and iron. Elaborate and costly
brooches of large size were used as the fastening of
the sagum.

British and Gaulish women wore a long pais, cotta,
or tunic reaching to the ankles, and over it a shorter
one, called the gwn, whence we get our modern word
gown. The sleeves of this latter garment reached only
to the elbow.

Fortunately for students of ancient British costume
the dress of Boadicea, Queen of the Iceni, has been
described by Dion Cassius. She wore a tunic of many
colours, all in folds, and over it, fastened by a fibula
or brooch, a robe of coarse stuff. Her light hair fell
loosely over her shoulders, and round her neck was a
golden torque. This necklace, or collar of twisted
wires of gold or silver, called torch or dorch in British,
was worn by both sexes in all the Celtic nations, and
was peculiarly a symbol of rank and command. So
fond were the ancient Britons of this kind of personal
adornment that those who could not procure them of
these precious metals wore them of brass and even
iron, and, according to the testimony of one writer, they
manifested no small amount of pride in displaying them.

There appear to have been three orders of the priesthood among the Britons before the period of the Roman occupation, viz.—

(i) The Druids, or sacerdotal order, who were clothed in white—the emblem of holiness, purity, and truth. A bas-relief found at Autun represents two Druids in long tunics and mantles, one crowned with an oaken garland and bearing a sceptre, the other holding in his hand a crescent, one of their sacred symbols. The mantle of the former is fastened on the left shoulder by a portion of it being drawn through a ring, and instances of this fashion, it may be remarked, are to be found subsequently in Anglo-Saxon costume. These rings have occasionally been found, and from their small size have been considered by some antiquaries to have served as votive bracelets.

(ii) The bards, who were the poets, the historians, and the genealogists of the Celtic nations, are supposed to have been clothed in long blue gowns.

(iii) The Ovates, professing astronomy and medicine, wore garments of green, the symbol of learning, because it was the colour of nature. The disciples of this order wore variegated dresses of three colours: white, blue, and green, according to one account, and blue, green, and red, according to another.

With regard to the military costume of the ancient Britons we possess some interesting information. Diodorus Siculus tells us that the Gauls wore upon the head helmets of brass, upon which were various appendages for the sake of ostentation, and also, it may be added, with a view of striking their antagonists with awe and fear by the exaggeration of their height and ferocious appearance. The feathers in the hair of the Red Indian and the hideous military masks of the Chinese were similar contrivances calculated to impress opponents in the field of battle. These Gaulish appendages to the helmet represented birds and beasts of various kinds. They were, in fact, the prototype of the mediæval crest. It is probable, although not absolutely certain, that the better equipped of the British soldiers were provided with helmets and appendages of this kind. The shields of the Britons were circular, or oblong, and flat. Those of circular form were only two feet in diameter, and had a hollow boss in the centre to admit the hand of the warrior who carried it. Shields of this kind were held at arm's length in action. They were formed internally of wicker, or basket-work; externally, the bronze face was ornamented with a number of concentric circles, between which were as large a number of little knobs as the space would permit.

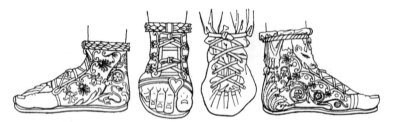

Roman shoes and sandals

CHAPTER II

ROMANO-BRITISH AND ANGLO-SAXON COSTUME

WITH the Roman occupation of Britain a new chapter in the history of costume begins, for the foreign influence was soon manifested in the style of personal attire and in many other departments of civil and official life. The Romans brought new ideas and new methods, and they unquestionably exerted a great civilizing force on the people who came under their sway. One writer has suggested that the nations of the ancient world might be fairly divided into two great groups or classes, the trousered and the untrousered. Amongst the latter were the Greeks and Romans, deriving their origin from the bare-legged Egyptians; while the two great branches of the Scythic or Northern Asiatic family, which had overrun Europe, and colonized the South of Britain long previous to the Roman invasion, viz., the Cimmerii and the Celtæ, wore the distinguishing close trousers or loose pantaloons called by them braccæ, or brachæ— the equivalent of the modern breeches. This important fact of ancient history may give a new meaning to that proverbial expression still so commonly used which relates to "wearing the breeches." It must be borne

in mind, however, that the ancient trousers or pantaloons were full and gathered about the ankle, and that
our modern trousers have during the past few centuries
passed through a quite independent series of modifications. Still, they are coverings for the legs, and the
ancient name is still applied to them.

The Romans set the fashion in England for many
centuries in reference to private or domestic dress, and
traces of a classic origin can be clearly seen in the
costumes of the Saxons and Danes.

A few words on the various garments of the Romans
may be useful.

Toga.—This was semicircular in shape, and worn so
as to form a kind of short sleeve to the right arm, and
to cover the left arm down to the wrist. A kind of
loop of folds was made to hang over the sloped drapery
in front, and the garment was sufficiently ample at the
back to enable it to be drawn over the head when
required. The toga was composed of wool, and
although sometimes worn in the natural colour, or
bleached, was dyed for the use of poor people, and
black in times of mourning.

Priests and magistrates wore the toga edged with a
purple border; knights wore the toga striped with
purple throughout; whilst the toga of a general was
entirely of purple, to which was added a rich embroidery of gold.

The toga was essentially a Roman garment, being
worn neither by the Greeks nor the barbarians. In
the earliest ages of Rome, it was worn by women as
well as men. In the course of time the use of the toga

ROMAN CIVILIAN IN BRITAIN, WEARING THE TOGA

FROM A SEPULCHRAL MONUMENT IN THE GUILDHALL MUSEUM, LONDON

RETIARIUS ON ROMAN SEPULCHRAL STONE IN THE GUILDHALL MUSEUM,
LONDON

became less general, but it was regularly worn on all state occasions.

TUNIC.—This garment was introduced at a later period than the toga, and was regarded as a kind of luxury. It reached, in the case of men, half-way down the thigh; but by women and effeminate men it was worn longer. The tunic, without the toga, was worn by soldiers in camp and by inferior functionaries at sacrifices. Senators wore a tunic edged with a purple border, called latus clavus; knights wore one with a narrow border.

MANTLE.—This garment, worn by soldiers over the armour and fastened on the right shoulder, was derived from the pallium, or mantle, of the Greeks. It was found to be less cumbersome than the toga, and therefore largely supplanted it.

HOODED CLOAK (Bardocucullus).—This was a garment of more purely utilitarian character than those just mentioned. It was made of very coarse brown wool, and was commonly worn by the people as a protection against cold and rough weather. Its hood (cucullus) was capable of being brought over the head in such a way as to throw off the rain, etc.

STOLA.—The under garment of the Roman ladies was a long tunic descending to the feet, called stola. Over it the palla (an adaptation of the Greek peplum) was sometimes worn.

Generally speaking, the dress of the Romans, during the earlier centuries of the Christian era, was plain, but after the middle of the fourth century A.D. a greater use of ornament makes its appearance, and fringes, tassels, and jewellery were worn in great profusion.

Two interesting pieces of Romano-British sculpture from London, and now in the Guildhall Museum, which are here figured, represent a Roman in civil dress wearing the toga, and a gladiator armed with a three-pointed lance and net. He is evidently represented as a retarius about to encounter his antagonist. The retarii, who generally wore a short tunic and no head-covering, and were armed with the trident, dagger, and net, fought by throwing the net so as to entangle the adversaries, whom they then attacked with their weapons.

Some of the tessellated pavements of the Romano-British period represent interesting costume, although, generally speaking, nude deities, nymphs, etc., are the favourite subjects. The pavements at Bignor, Sussex, a part of which is here shown, represent one or two curious groups of humorous gladiatorial conflicts.

ANGLO-SAXON COSTUME

The period which is included under this head extends from the withdrawal of the Romans from Britain in or about 436 A.D. to the Norman Conquest in 1066. Of the earlier half of this period very little is known. No reliable contemporary picture or manuscript exists to illuminate what is one of the darkest chapters of English history.

The contents of Anglo-Saxon graves, however, give some extremely valuable information regarding certain

COSTUMES OF ROMANO-BRITISH GLADIATORS

(FROM MOSAIC PAVEMENTS AT BIGNOR, SUSSEX)

parts of the ornaments which were worn by the people of the time.

What is believed to have been the earliest method of burying the dead in use amongst the Anglo-Saxons was performed in the following manner : the dead body was fully dressed and furnished with arms, such as circular hide-covered shields with iron bosses, knife or knives, sword, spear, etc., in the same manner as in life, and then wrapped in an ample winding-sheet and placed in the grave without any further protection than a few large stones. This method of burial was very generally followed by the Jutes, who resided in Kent, Hampshire, and the Isle of Wight, as many of the graves in the extensive Kentish cemeteries clearly prove. In some cases, however, traces of stone and wooden coffins have been noticed.[1]

The graves of Anglo-Saxon ladies have furnished our museums and private collections with numerous examples of the jewellery and personal ornaments which were so much in vogue amongst our ancestors. These consist of glass beads of various colours, beads of amber and other stones, ornamental combs made of bone, hairpins made of metals, and sometimes enriched with slices of garnet, and brooches or fibulæ of a great variety of forms, sizes, and degrees of elaboration. The fibulæ are perhaps the most important of all the ornaments, from the fact that distinct types can be clearly recognized, and the diffusion of tribes by that means can be traced.

[1] Akerman, J. Y., *Remains of Pagan Saxondom*, pp. xv-xvi.

What the actual clothes were which the Anglo-Saxons wore during the pagan period is a matter upon which not much reliable evidence is available. Fragments of textiles have been found in a good many graves, usually adhering to oxidized or corroded objects of metal, or cemented to the bones or other objects by metallic oxides, but anything like a complete garment is wanting.

Judging from the contemporary costume of the Franks (who had overrun a part of France as the Saxons overran England), we are able to form an idea of what the early Anglo-Saxon costume was, for it is known that there was some resemblance between the dress of the two peoples.

A writer of the fifth century, in describing the dress of some Franks whom he saw enter the city of Lyons, in 470, says they were attired in a closely-fitting body garment, terminating above the knees, with exceedingly short sleeves, scarcely covering the shoulders, and made of some striped material not specified. Over this tunic, for such it was, they wore a sagum of greenish colour with a scarlet border. They were girt with a broad belt ornamented with metal bosses or studs, and wore their swords suspended on the left side by a baldric crossing their breast. Their thighs and legs were entirely bare, but they had laced boots of undressed leather reaching to the ankles. They had a very strange custom of shaving the backs of their heads completely, leaving their front hair to grow to a great length and piling it on the top of their heads so as to form a knot. They also shaved their faces closely, leaving

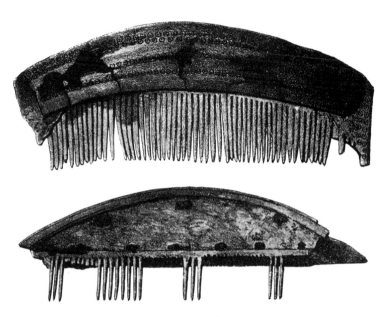

ANGLO-SAXON COMBS

ANGLO-SAXON BROOCHES

only very small whiskers. The absence of leg-coverings is an interesting trace of Roman civilization.

Turning now to the Anglo-Saxon costume at this time, there is reason to believe, as we have just said, that it bore considerable marks of similarity to the Frankish. The earliest Anglo-Saxon MS. in the British Museum, of clearly ascertained date, is the beautiful copy of the Gospels, known as "The Durham Book," having been written by Eadfrid, Bishop of Durham, and illuminated by his successor, Bishop Ethelwold, about the year 720. This MS., however, contains only representations of the four Evangelists, copied apparently from some of the paintings brought over by early missionaries, and therefore useless as evidences of Anglo-Saxon costume.

During the last century of the Anglo-Saxon period we have numerous MSS., authorities on the costume of the time, and these all confirm the belief that the Anglo-Saxons in England closely resembled in costume the Franks of France.

The shirt is said, upon good authority, to have been a garment commonly worn by the Anglo-Saxons as early as the eighth century, although it is not easily distinguished from the short tunic. It was, of course, worn next the skin, and consequently was not usually represented in drawings. It appears to have fitted more closely to the body than the tunic, and the folds of the sleeves, from the elbow to the wrist, seem to have been much smaller than they are generally in the tunic. The material of which the shirt was made was probably white linen.

The tunic in Anglo-Saxon times was of two kinds, viz. the short tunic worn at times by all classes of people, and the long tunic, which is generally understood to have been the distinguishing mark of superior rank. The short tunic may be described as closely resembling the modern shirt. It was apparently put upon the body over the head in the same manner, and the aperture at the top is sometimes drawn no larger than barely sufficient to admit the passing through of the head; but at other times it is seen open upon the bosom, and adorned with a border. This garment was sometimes open from the hip downwards on either side, and in that form it seems to have been the distinguishing badge of slavery or servitude. When the tunic was not slit at the sides the wearer was a freeman.

Short tunics were universally worn by all classes of society, but the long tunic appears to have been worn by persons of the most exalted rank, and then only on state days or other solemn occasions.

The sleeves of the long tunic were sometimes loose and open, but sometimes they fitted tightly to the arms; but they seem always to have reached to the wrist. The garment was bound about the waist with a girdle, and descended in loose, graceful folds to the feet. It was usually white, probably of linen, but sometimes it was of different colours.

This supertunic, or surcoat as it is sometimes called, was worn over the tunic by persons of rank. The most important garment to be noticed next, however, is the cloak or mantle, an article of dress worn by both sexes in all ages. The sagum of the Ancient Britons became the cloak or mantle of the Anglo-Saxons. It was usually fastened by means of a fibula or buckle over the right shoulder in such a way as to give perfect freedom of action to the right arm. The cloak descended to a little below the skirts of the short tunic, and, covering all the back, it was gathered into sloping folds over the left arm and part of the breast. In some instances, however, the cloak was fastened by a buckle over the left shoulder, and in the case of the nobility it was often fastened upon the breast with a fibula, and being more ample in its dimensions, it covered both shoulders.

In these different ways of wearing the cloak or mantle a sufficiently large opening appears to have been always left for the garment to be quickly thrown off over the head. Some forms seem to have been rarely represented in which no buckle at all was used, a hole being made in the middle of the garment for the passage of the head. This is by some supposed to have been a form of cloak specially designed for winter wear. There was still another variety of mantle which was bound about the waist, and reached below the knees, while the other part of it, passing over the left or right shoulder, covered the back, and descended to the middle of the leg. This form was used especially by the king and the nobles of the period.

The wooden model of a boat containing warriors found at Roos Carrs, near Withernsea, now in the museum at Hull, may be mentioned here. It is of great importance as a relic of ancient Scandinavian art, probably of the Viking period, and imported into this country.   Unfortunately for our purpose the warriors are all nude, although one bears a circular shield as a defence against his enemies.

The costumes of the tenth and eleventh centuries are admirably illustrated in illuminated MSS. of that period, several good examples of which are in the British Museum.

In Harleian MS. 2886, for example, there are two warriors roughly sketched.   One is in the act of despatching his antagonist, a prostrate and nude man. The other is engaged in slaying a dragon.   In both cases diamond-shaped spear-heads are employed.   In each case the dress is practically the same.   It consists of a short tunic extending to a point only a little below the knees and mainly hidden by an over-garment reaching from the neck to the waist, with close-fitting sleeves extending quite to the wrists and considerably wrinkled about the arms.   An outer mantle of loose character, and apparently of moderately thick material, is fastened over the right shoulder and hangs down on the left side, where it is caught up again somewhat by the left arm. The fastening of the mantle on the right shoulder is large and of curious shape.   It is clearly a kind of metal brooch, and decidedly larger than one might consider necessary.   It may be described as of an oblong shape, the longer sides being incurved or concave.   There is a species of boss or pin in the middle. The large size and prominent character of these brooches recall the very large and elaborate fibulæ of which the pagan Saxons were so fond at an earlier period.

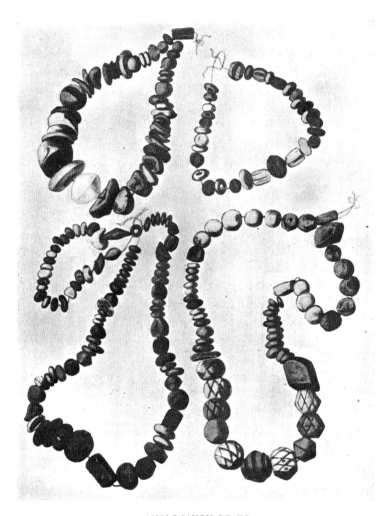

ANGLO-SAXON BEADS

Below the over-garment just described an ornamental pouch or scrip is seen on the right-hand side of the wearer.

There are one or two strongly marked characteristics of the costume of the tenth and eleventh centuries, namely, (1) the hose is composed of thin materials, so that it falls in wrinkles on the lower part of the leg; (2) mantles are generally short and fastened by a more or less prominent brooch or buckle over the right shoulder; and (3) fighting men are furnished with long spears.

On making a comparison of the evidence afforded by illuminated MSS. as to the costumes worn in the latter part of the Anglo-Saxon period and that furnished by sepulchral and other remains of the dress of the earlier Anglo-Saxon period, we find resemblances on certain points which are decidedly important. Both brooches and spear-heads are regularly found in Anglo-Saxon graves of the pagan period. The mantle was doubtless generally worn during the earlier period, and was fastened by elaborately ornamented brooches. These brooches or fibulæ are the most important and constant of the metallic ornaments found amongst Anglo-Saxon remains; and from the fact that they were frequently enriched with gilding and stones, and were of large size, we may infer that they were worn as ornaments on an outer garment, where they would be constantly visible. The brooches, when found in graves, are sometimes in pairs, usually on the breast, where it is probable they had been placed to fasten the mantle in which the dead body was wrapped when buried.

The well-known British Museum MS., Harl. 603, is of great value on account of the evidence it furnishes for the English costume of the eleventh century, to which period and country it belongs. The various garments are coloured in outline in such a manner as to enable one to distinguish quite clearly between them. Generally speaking, we can gather from this that (1) the legs are bare ; (2) the chief garment may be described as a loosely fitting, long-sleeved tunic, covering the body from the neck only to the mid-thigh ; (3) the outer garment is a small mantle or cape, fastened by means of a globular brooch or button on the top of the right shoulder of the wearer and falling down only to about the elbow of the left arm or a little beyond. Some of the fighting men are furnished with shoes, wrinkled stockings reaching only from the mid-calf downwards, and long spears. The houses, bedsteads, ships, cups, vessels, casks, and many other objects represented are of the greatest antiquarian interest.

Another British Museum MS. of Prudentius, *De Pugna Vitiorum* (Add. MS. 24,199), gives us some interesting pictures of eleventh century fighting men wearing short tunics furnished with long, close-fitting sleeves and loosely setting mantles fastened at the right shoulder and falling in front a little below the waist and also over the left arm. The caps they wear are distinctly curious, fitting round the head quite tightly like nightcaps and ending in curved, horn-like points, which remind one of the Phrygian cap or the head-dress worn as typical of liberty, etc., at the

French Revolution, the only difference being that the curved points are supported by a vertical and apparently stiff band reaching from the forehead to the apex of the cap.

The mounted soldiers are furnished with rather elaborately pointed spears.

In Julius A. vi. (British Museum MS.) we have an interesting series of pen-and-ink drawings illustrating scenes in rural English life. There is a curious little picture for each month, viz. :—

January—ploughing.
February—pruning trees.
March—digging and raking the soil.
April—feasting.
May—tending sheep.
June—felling timber and carting it away.
July—reaping grass with scythes.
August—reaping corn with sickles or hooks ; harvest-cart.
September—tending swine.
October—hawking.
November—burning wood, and building (?).
December—threshing corn and taking it away in large basket of primitive character.

Throughout these scenes the workmen are shown wearing tunics, probably girded or belted, with no mantle nor cape nor head-dress, but furnished with shoes and short, wrinkled stockings.

The beautiful Benedictional of St. Æthelwold affords some valuable evidence as to the tenth century. A benedictional, it is perhaps hardly necessary to say, is a book containing rites of benediction believed to have been used by a bishop exclusively during Mass. It was an ancient custom for the bishop, on the fraction of the Host, to bless the people in the form of prayer appropriate to the day. This benediction, given just before the bishop had communicated, was read from the benedictional.

The particular copy known as that of St. Æthelwold was written by Godemann the monk, made abbot of Thorney about 970. It was written for St. Æthelwold, who was Bishop of Winchester from 963 to 984. The book is the property of the Duke of Devonshire, and was described and illustrated in the twenty-fourth volume of *Archæologia*.

The richness of the illuminations of the manuscript, and the fact that they were almost certainly painted by an English artist, give it a special value as evidence for the costume of the period.

The preliminary miniatures in the MS. represent confessors, virgins, apostles, etc., all drawn with great skill and delicacy. The draperies, which are obviously of thin materials, hang in graceful folds to the feet of the figures of the virgins, and to the ankles in those of the apostles, etc. In both sexes the robes are loosely confined round the waists by a broad band or girdle of soft, thin material, which is drawn into folds by the slight tension resulting from use round the waist. The robes themselves are ample, and so large as to require generally to be held up in the hand, either right or left, or to be thrown over the arm in loose folds.

Perhaps the most interesting of the whole series of pictures is the last, which portrays a bishop in the act

ST. ÆTHELWOLD GIVING THE BENEDICTION
(TENTH CENTURY MASS-VESTMENTS)

of giving the benediction to the people assembled within a church. The bishop, probably intended as a representation of St. Æthelwold himself, is here shown as wearing a blue chasuble with gold border and gold apparel of the amice. The stole is likewise of gold colour, whilst the dalmatic is of striped material coloured perpendicularly red, blue, and white. The special point for notice, however, is the thin material and ample size of the chasuble, the former being well indicated by the folds and creases caused by the uplifted arm, and the latter being abundantly shown by the fact that the chasuble reaches quite to the wrists.

Of the various scenes represented, that showing our Lord's entry into Jerusalem is specially noteworthy on account, not only of the costume, but also for its representations of the gateway and houses of Jerusalem. The details of the harness of the ass on which our Lord rides are also well shown.

The Bodleian manuscript, commonly known as Cædmon's *Metrical Paraphrase of Scripture History*, is believed to be a work of quite the end of the tenth century, or possibly the first year or two of the eleventh century ; the date 1000 is that to which the best authorities agree in assigning it.

Cædmon has been designated the father of English poetry. He was certainly a most remarkable man, and deserves far more attention than he has hitherto received. For the present purpose, however, the chief interest lies in the illustrations which depict scenes in the fall of a portion of the angelic host, the creation and fall of man, the histories of Cain and Abel, and of the prophets, etc., both before and after the Flood.

The trees and vegetation, which are freely introduced into the scenes in the Garden of Eden, are treated in a semi-conventional, semi-naturalistic style which affords evidence of great skill and artistic feeling.

The garments worn by Adam and Eve after the expulsion from Eden are slight, and in the case of Adam only reach to the thighs. Eve, however, wears a kirtle-like under-garment, a gown reaching below the knees, with fairly loose sleeves, and an ample kerchief falling over the shoulders and turned back over the brow. There is a touch of delicate pathos in the scene : Adam goes forth as a workman, equipped with spade and basket for tilling the soil ; and Eve, with troubled face, follows, her left hand placed near her husband's arm, her right hand still grasping one of the apples from the tree in the Garden.

In the scenes representing the story of Cain and Abel we find that shoes are worn, and the legs are partially covered with loose, wrinkled stockings, which in some cases reach only half-way up to the knees. For digging the soil the regular single-shouldered spade is used.

The picture showing Tubal-Cain is of great value because it gives representations of him (i) playing upon the lyre, (ii) working as a smith at the anvil, and (iii) ploughing. In addition to the great interest of having the exact forms of implements in use in England at the end of the tenth century, these three scenes give a good idea of the costumes worn by artificers and hus-

SCENES FROM THE LIFE OF ST. GUTHLAC

bandmen at that period. In each case the skirts are gathered up round the waist so as to avoid the pollution of the forge and the plough furrow, and in each case also, apparently, a kind of thick leather apron is worn to protect the garments.

CHAPTER III

NORMAN COSTUME

THE chief source of information on the costume of Normandy and England a little before and a little after the period of the Norman Conquest is to be found in the remarkable piece of needlework known as the Bayeux Tapestry. The very large numbers of representations of people of various ranks, and performing different duties, would alone serve to give a special value to it, as the traditional record of its having been worked by Matilda, the queen of the Conqueror, gives it great historic interest. Moreover, it is apparent, on comparing it with manuscript sources, that its details are to a very large extent reliable. One striking peculiarity about the Norman soldiers who accompanied William was the curious fashion of shaving the back of the head as well as the hairy parts of the face. The custom, which was of considerable antiquity, gave rise to the idea amongst the English that the Duke of Normandy had brought over with him an army of priests rather than soldiers.

In process of time the Normans began to wear rich and flowing garments, and the hair of the head and beard were also permitted to flourish. The costume of the actual labourers or serfs of this period was, how-

ever, quite simple. Husbandmen were dressed in
simple tunics, without girdles, and furnished with
close-fitting sleeves, and they also wore the mantle
fastened over the right shoulder so as to have the right

King Harold seated on the throne with Archbishop Stigand on his
left hand

arm free for action. Their hats seem to have been
made of some soft material, and of quite simple form,
with somewhat pointed top and turned-up brim, much
like the hats now worn by farm-labourers.

The middle-class Normans wore long tunics reaching nearly to the ankles. Sometimes these were of

white material with a red lining. These tunics were often open on the left side from the waist downwards so as to expose nearly the whole of the left leg, which was covered with a close-fitting garment above and with banded stockings, or bandages, below the knee. In at least one illumination (Brit. Mus. MS., Cotton., Nero, C, 4) there is a representation of a stocking reaching above the knee, where apparently it has been

Norman soldiers wearing mantles
(Bayeux tapestry)

rolled back. In the same figure (which, by the way, is intended for Noah with his hatchet about to build the Ark) the shoes are ornamented by diagonal lines crossing each other.

The dress of the Norman ladies represents a development of that of the ladies of the Anglo-Saxon period. One of the first changes is in the appearance of a long, pendulous lappet from the under side of the sleeve close to the wrist. This grew sometimes to a length of more than a yard, and suggests the long liripipe of

later times. The colours of the sleeves, too, generally
varied from those of the materials of the gowns, which
were flowing and ample. Trains were much worn by
Norman ladies, and occasionally we see them shown
as tied up in knots. The waists were well cared for

Armed and mounted followers of Duke William (William the Conqueror)
(From the Bayeux tapestry)

and kept in proper shape by means of lacing. The
hair was allowed to grow very long and was plaited.

The earliest Norman kings, as shown by the great
seals, wore a tunic reaching below the knees, and a
mantle fastened by means of a brooch on the front of
the right shoulder. The swords and orbs surmounted
by the cross, which they also carry, are hardly parts of
their costume.

The vestments worn by Archbishop Stigand (1052–

D

70), as shown in the Bayeux Tapestry, are remarkable for their comparatively plain character, and the front of the chasuble is curiously short.

The typical Norman soldier wore a hauberk, or military tunic of chain mail, which fitted the body closely, and was slit a little way up in front and behind for the convenience of riding. Meyrick, in referring to this garment, gives the following explanation :—

It appears to have been put on by first drawing it on the thighs, where it sits wide, and then putting the arms into the sleeves, which hang loosely, reaching not much above the elbow, as was the case with the Saxon flat-ringed tunic. The hood attached to it was then brought up over the head, and the opening on the chest covered by a square piece, through which were passed straps that fastened behind, hanging down with tasselled terminations, as did also the strap which drew the hood, or capuchon, as it was called, tight round the forehead. The legs were protected by ringed mail, and the head by a conical helmet with well-developed nose-guard.

An interesting episode relating to the dress worn by Thomas à Becket, before he accepted the primacy, is recorded by William Fitz-Stephen as follows :—

He (Thomas à Becket) was sitting one day at the [game of] Exchequer, dressed in a cape with sleeves. Archetinus, Prior of Leicester, came to see him, coming from the King's Court, who was in Gascony at that time, who speaking to him freely, relying on their familiarity, said to him, "Why do we use a cape with sleeves? That dress belongs more to those who carry hawks; but you are an ecclesiastical

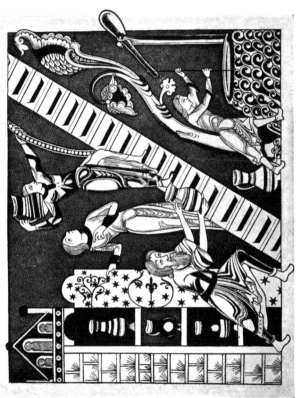

TWELFTH CENTURY COSTUME

(COTT. MS. NERO C. IV, BRIT. MUS.)

person, one in singularity, but several in dignity : Arch-
deacon of Canterbury, Dean of Hastings, Provost of Bever-
ley, a Canon here and there, an Archiepiscopal proctor, and,
as rumour very frequently is current at Court, you will be
Archbishop."

CHAPTER IV

THIRTEENTH CENTURY COSTUME

THIRTEENTH century costume is remarkable for its simplicity and grace. This is due, perhaps, to the use of fine and gracefully falling materials quite as much as to simplicity of fashion. Such ornaments as orphreys or applied enrichment were used more sparingly, but the actual fabrics were probably of more costly character than before. Something of the beauty of existing representations of thirteenth century garments is unquestionably due to the good taste and delicate treatment of the artists of the period; but an age that produced such good artists could hardly fail to produce also good costume makers; and the hands which were capable of producing such beautiful pictures of clinging folds were certainly able to produce and appreciate the original garments.

That this refinement is due to a foreign (probably French) influence, no one who has studied the art of the two kingdoms can doubt. The miniatures show a species of skill in the delineation of the features, the drawing of the hair and beard, and in the general treatment, which came almost certainly from France.

One of the important sources of information as to the civil and military costume of England during the

A KNIGHT TEMPLAR
(TEMPLE CHURCH, LONDON)

earlier half of the thirteenth century is *Vitæ duorum Offarum*, a manuscript work generally attributed to Matthew Paris. The manuscript, which is now in the British Museum (Cott. MS., Nero, D, i.), is embellished with a number of miniatures depicting scenes in the lives of Offa I and Offa II. They are believed by

Knights in chain-mail fighting (thirteenth century)
(From the *Lives of the Two Offas*)

some authorities to have been actually drawn by Matthew Paris, although doubts have been thrown both on this point and on the authorship of the text.[1]

Many of the pictures from the manuscript have been published in outline in Strutt's *Manners, Customs, Arms, Habits, etc., of the Inhabitants of England,*

[1] See article on Matthew Paris in the *Dictionary of National Biography.*

Vol. I. They are simply invaluable for our present purpose. One of the striking things they teach is the simplicity and similarity of English costume at this period. As Mr. Oswald Barron, F.S.A. (*The Ancestor*, V. 100) has pointed out, kings, lords, churchmen, and men of condition wear long

Sweyn slain by Offa.   (From a thirteenth century MS., the
Lives of the Two Offas)

gowns to the feet, ornamented for great folk with orphreys or bands of embroidery at the neck, which is cut somewhat low. The first series shows a fashion of sleeve with wide ends cut off at the mid-forearm, and showing the tight sleeve of a smock or other garment below. Some of the late pictures show the sleeves ending at the wrists. A notable point about all the sleeves shown in this manuscript is that the upper part in every case is cut widely, and has a

EFFIGY OF KING JOHN. WORCESTER CATHEDRAL

curiously large armhole, reaching in some cases
almost to the waist. Over this gown is worn an
ample cloak, which sometimes bears a hood, fastened
at the neck with a brooch or band.

The dress of the common folk and of men of rank

Offa II crowned king of the Mercians. (From a
thirteenth century MS.)

when actively employed is a like gown or coat ending
at the knee, with which is worn a shorter cloak also to
the knee. The belts or girdles which gird the coats
and gowns at the knee appear as plain thongs; they
give no indication of the rich buckles and heavy bosses
which soon afterwards came into fashion.

The head-dresses are well worthy of careful attention. They comprise caps, hats, hoods, and coifs. The hood covering head and neck is not shown as worn over the head except in the case of the humbler folk. The common headgear in warfare is the coif of mail. Barrel helms, and iron caps fitted with nose-guards of the ancient fashion, are also found. Except for the head-pieces no plates appear beyond greaves, or bainbergs and small knee-caps.

It is worthy of remark that the ordinary dress of the churchmen was the same as that of the laymen, except for their curious caps.

Several important details of military costume or armour are given in some of the scenes. Chain mail encases the entire bodies of the warriors, but knee-caps and greaves are worn. In one interesting example (here figured) a knight, who has been struck in the neck by a spear, wears a mask of plate strengthened and ornamented with a cross boutonnée. There is no iron cap on the knight's head in this case, although in others such head-defences, and sometimes furnished with nose-guards, are depicted. Other kinds of iron caps are conical in form, with a more or less developed point at the top.

EFFIGY OF KING EDWARD II

CHAPTER V

FOURTEENTH CENTURY COSTUME

THE reign of Edward II, which began quite early in the fourteenth century (1307), was a period of great extravagance in dress. Edward II himself was noted for his luxuriousness in this respect, and his favourites about the Court were effeminate and dissipated. It was in the Royal Court of England, during this monarch's twenty years' reign, that many of the fantastic and novel fashions in dress, for which the fourteenth century became famous, were introduced. At first confined to the Court circle, the fashions in time grew into popularity all over the land.

Fairholt, in *Costume in England*, remarks that the apparel of Edward II, as represented in the sepulchral effigy at Gloucester, displays none of the luxuriousness for which that monarch was famous; but this seems hardly remarkable when it is remembered that the King is represented, not in the gay attire of everyday life, but in his coronation robes, which from their official and sacred character could not be expected to reflect the follies and fashions of the time.

Whatever may be the evidence of sepulchral effigies as to the plainness of the dress of certain distinguished individuals, there is no possibility of mistaking the evidence of the effigies and monumental brasses of humbler folk. Of this kind of illustration of English costume our old churches afford much that is of the greatest value. It is, perhaps, impossible to find a more pleasing occupation, for such as are keenly interested in costume, than the collecting of evidence, in the form of rubbings, photographs, or drawings, of the various garments worn by men and women of different stations of life, or engaged in trade, etc. This is, perhaps, particularly true of the fourteenth century because of the great beauty and merit of the figures, whether engraved on plates of metal, in the form familiarly known as monumental brasses, or in the round, in the shape of sepulchral effigies. Moreover, it was the custom to represent costume of this period with great precision and vigour.

Fortunately, the evidence for fourteenth century costume is not confined to effigies. We have illuminated manuscripts and verbal descriptions as well as literary references.

William of Malmesbury, the chronicler, tells us that, at the beginning of the fourteenth century, "The esquire endeavoured to outshine the knight, the knight the baron, the baron the earl, the earl the King himself, in the richness of his apparel."

There were two great changes in the costume of the fourteenth century introduced as innovations, and not peculiar to England, but common to the continent of Europe. These were (i) the introduction of particoloured dress, and (ii) the custom of wearing lappets hanging from the elbows. Planché, in his *Cyclopædia of Costume*, regards these two new fashions as characteristic of fourteenth century costume.

The use of parti-colours in dress is attributed to the increasing popularity of heraldry at this period, and the very natural custom of servants and retainers being furnished with clothes of the heraldic colours of their masters seems to have been very generally followed as a popular custom, without any special significance being intended.

The cote-hardie, or close-fitting tunic reaching to the middle, and furnished with tight sleeves, may be said to be a characteristic fourteenth century garment. Over it was worn by the wealthy a broad, jewelled girdle with dagger and pouch. This girdle appears to rest on the hips, but in reality it was attached by means of hooks to the tunic. Shoes and long, parti-coloured hose covered the feet and legs.

It will be convenient at this point, before proceeding to consider the general costume of the people, to glance at some of the contemporary sources of information, beginning with some good examples of fourteenth century illuminations in manuscripts.

Some important examples of the fourteenth century costumes of servants, both domestic and agricultural, are to be found in the Louttrell Psalter, an illuminated manuscript, executed for Sir Geoffrey Louttrell, knight, about the year 1330. The great value of these pictures is that, in addition to some representing tumblers, jugglers, etc., in the main they depict the occupations of cooking and serving up joints for the table, also ploughing, sowing, harrowing, weeding, reaping,

threshing, corn-grinding, spinning, archery, and a
number of other games, in which the men and women
are clad in attire which is obviously the regular dress
of the period.

The great variety of head-dress represented is one
of the features of the manuscript, and, although there
are many garments upon which it furnishes valuable
information, the head-coverings are perhaps the most
prominent and varied.   Indeed the Louttrell Psalter
gives us a perfect epitome of the dress worn by the
working classes of England during the earlier half of
the fourteenth century.   Most of the authorities on
mediæval dress give details of fine and sumptuous
garments only, such as would be worn by royal and
noble personages ; the importance of a storehouse of
facts relating to the dress of the lower orders, such as
this, is therefore, of course, very great.

In the accompanying reproductions of portions of
the manuscripts are shown—

(i) A labouring man and woman engaged in breaking
up clods of soil by means of long-handled mallets.
The man wears a girdled tunic, a head-dress enveloping the head and neck, and falling in a kind of liripipe
behind, and boots with leggings, probably in the form
of bandages, reaching half-way between the foot and
the knee.   The woman has a simple gown, ornamental
belt, apron, and head-dress much like the man.   Neither
wear gloves.

(ii) A ploughman and his "mate" engaged in
ploughing with a team of oxen.   The ploughman
wears a head-dress similar to the labourer just described,

BREAKING CLODS OF EARTH WITH MALLETS

PLOUGHING

RURAL COSTUME, FROM THE LOUTERELL PSALTER
(FOURTEENTH CENTURY)

and over it a kind of seaman's "south-wester" hat. His tunic, boots, etc., are also similar, but he has a girdle pierced with eyelet-holes, from which hangs an object, possibly a knife. The "mate," driving the

oxen with a long whip, is somewhat similarly clothed, but wears, over all, an outer garment of leather. The plough is interesting as showing most of the features of the more modern, but now almost obsolete, turn-rise plough.

(iii) Cooks and servers, engaged in preparing viands and conveying them to the table. The cook wears a head-dress very similar to those of the men just described, but the part for the covering of the neck and throat is thrown up, and the liripipe-like point is tilted forward. The servers wore belted tunics, but no head-gear.

Nicholas de Aum-
berdene, about
1350 (Taplow,
Bucks)

The dress of civilians in the earlier part of the fourteenth century is shown by the effigies on several monumental brasses. The example here shown is that of Nicholas de Aumberdene, about 1350, at Taplow, Buckinghamshire. The dress consists of (1) a close-fitting tunic, or cote-hardie, reaching below the knees, with the pockets in front, and with sleeves reaching to the elbows, from which point they hang down as long lappets or liripipes; (2) an under-dress, of which the tight-fitting sleeves seen on the forearms are the only visible parts ; and (3) a hood covering the shoulders, attached to which is a cape or tippet. The legs, it may be added, are clothed in tight hose, and the feet are protected by shoes. Shoes during this century, it may be remarked, were usually laced up at the sides, or fastened across the instep.

A British Museum manuscript which illustrates the subject of English costume in the early part of the fourteenth century is that known as *Royal MS.*, 19 B, xv., containing the Apocalypse of St. John written in the French language, but the miniatures as well as the caligraphy are the work of English hands.

This manuscript shows that the civil costume of the period was decidedly simple, the gowns falling in graceful lines to the ankles without girdles, and the hats composed of soft materials, and so made as to be comfortable to the head. The necks of the gowns and coats are cut somewhat low. In one picture of a lady we have a white wimple and kerchief, the latter arranged on the head so that one end falls over and hangs down from the left-hand side of the head in a way suggestive of the liripipe of later times. Some of the men wear conical caps of white colour with a green turned-up brim. The soft material of which the pointed centre of the caps is composed is well indicated, and suggests similar head-dresses worn by the peasantry which afterwards developed into liripipes, which are so well illustrated in the illuminations of the Louttrell Psalter. As far as military costume is concerned, the manuscript shows us few startling novelties. Generally hauberks

COOK AND SERVERS. LOUTERELL PSALTER

of banded mail reaching a little below the knees and continuing without visible joints into close hoods of mail. The head is protected by iron hats of rather wide bell-like form, but close-fitting skull-caps of iron are also worn. Another decidedly curious species of head protection worn consists of a kind of framework of iron taking the form of four curved ribs connecting the apex with the brim, and disclosing below it a cap of some soft, coloured material.

Fortunately, some of the pictures show execution scenes, in which the victims are only partially clothed. These enable us to see that the shirts worn by the men were low and plain at the neck, with short and loose sleeves descending only to the elbows, while the whole garment reached to the knees, and was slit up slightly at the sides. In one case a victim is shown wearing a combination garment uniting the features of shirt and drawers.

Another MS. in the British Museum (Royal MS., 14 E, iii.), containing the story of the Quest of the Holy Grail, contains pictures which have an important bearing on the costume at the period when they were executed, namely, the earlier half of the fourteenth century. The pictures were probably drawn by French artists.

In the military figures ailettes are worn in nearly every case. They first made their appearance during the last quarter of the thirteenth century, and they remained in fashion throughout the first quarter of the fourteenth century—in other words, for a period of about fifty years. As Mr. Oswald Barron has pointed out in *The Ancestor* :—[1]

. . . Fastened by laces and tags to the back or side of the shoulder, they filled several uses. They helped to cover the weak spot at the armpit which the knight who would use his arms freely must perforce have ill protected. Like the high-ridged plates of a later period, they offered some defence against a sweeping sword blow at the neck, and, above all, they offered a new field for the work of the arms-painter. Were they not sometimes found unemblazoned this last reason might have been pressed as the main argument for their use. That their adornment was sometimes of the richest is shown by the inventory of the goods of the wretched Piers de Gavaston, who owned alettes garnished and fretted with pearls. Their shape is usually square or oblong, but the round and other shapes have been noted.

Most of the knights in this manuscript are shown armed from head to foot in mail, not in plate armour. Their head defences are generally of round, basin-shaped form, and some wear the great helm, strengthened by bars and stays, and with a high pointed top. There are no instances of crests worn on the helms. Two knights are furnished with the latest fashion in head-pieces, a bascinet with a movable vizor, which is represented as pushed back over the crown of the bascinet.

The Society of Antiquaries of London possesses, amongst many other pictures of great value for the student of English costume, a series of four paintings on two wooden panels representing scenes in the life of

[1] Vol. VIII, p. 146.

SECOND MARRIAGE OF ST. ETHELDREDA (ST. AUDRY) TO THE KING OF
NORTHUMBRIA
(LATE FOURTEENTH CENTURY COSTUME)

ST. ETHELDREDA IN MONASTIC GOWN AND CROWN
(LATE FOURTEENTH CENTURY COSTUME)

St. Etheldreda. The paintings, which are executed with great spirit in oil colours with a charming background of patterned gesso-work, are probably of the end of the fourteenth century. They are traditionally stated to have belonged to Ely Cathedral, where they probably served as the doors of an aumbry or cupboard. St. Etheldreda, of course, was a local saint. She had a convent on the very site afterwards occupied by Ely Cathedral. This was destroyed by the Northmen, and the body of the saint was translated from the old Saxon to the new building, finished by Abbot Richard early in the twelfth century. A series of paintings representing scenes in the strange life-history of Etheldreda, painted for use in Ely Cathedral, may probably have special significance; and if the panels were not used to enclose her actual relics, they may have been intended as doors for securing clothing or other souvenirs of the Saxon queen.

Whatever may have been the use of these painted doors, there can be no question as to the beauty of the pictures and the high degree of interest they have for our present purpose.

In the left-hand upper picture we have a representation of the second formal marriage of St. Etheldreda to Egfrid, King of Northumbria. Ten persons appear in the picture, of whom the King and Queen and officiating bishop are the most important. The King wears a girded robe of baudekin, over which is a dark mantle, lined, edged, and caped with ermine. He is attended by a noble dressed in a similar robe and wearing a red mantle with ermine lining and cape.

E

The next subject, to the right of the above, consists of a group of six figures. The King has a long scarlet robe with a large pouch hanging from his girdle. The Queen (St. Etheldreda), who still wears her crown, has assumed a monastic garb, consisting of a black mantle or robe, lined and edged with ermine, possibly a wimple, and a kerchief or veil over her head. She is evidently about to retire to the abbey of Coldingham. The ladies who attend her wear turban-like head-dresses, but their robes are not of a monastic character.

In the third picture St. Etheldreda, in monastic dress, crowned, and carrying a book in the right hand, is inspecting the building of the church at Ely. Masons, in canvas or leather aprons, are busy squaring, shaping, and setting the blocks of stone. Mortar for the purpose is contained in shallow, bow-like vessels, and the several tools they are using, which are well shown, comprise hammer or adze, set-square, callipers or compasses, and axe.

The fourth and last picture represents the translation in 695 of the incorrupt body of the saint, vested as before. Four nuns carefully place the body in the Roman sarcophagus. A bishop (possibly intended as a portrait of Archbishop Chicheley), vested in a magnificent chasuble of baudekin, with an attendant priest carrying his staff, officiates or directs.

The translation of St. Etheldreda (17th October) is an interesting day in many respects. Formerly it was the custom to celebrate it by a fair at which cheap fancy objects were offered for sale to country people. The day of this fair came, by a simple process of

ST. ETHELDREDA BUILDS THE CHURCH AT ELY

(LATE FOURTEENTH CENTURY COSTUME)

THE TRANSLATION OF ST. ETHELDREDA
(LATE FOURTEENTH CENTURY COSTUME)

abbreviation, to be called St. Awdry's Day, and the English word "tawdry," as descriptive of cheap, gaudy wares, took its rise from the circumstance.

These paintings, which may be regarded as admirable illustrations of late fourteenth century costume, etc., differ in a considerable degree from the legend of St. Etheldreda, as sculptured in stone in Ely Cathedral, in which no less than eight scenes are depicted; but it is quite possible that the panels now in the possession of the Society of Antiquaries[1] do not represent a complete series.

The beautiful effigy of Sir John de Creke (here reproduced) and of his lady (shown on page 146) exist side by side on the monumental brass; they illustrate the great beauty and refinement in the dress of wealthy people during the first quarter of the fourteenth century. In the case of the lady it will be seen

Sir John de Creke, about 1325 (Westley Waterless, Cambridgeshire)

[1] The accompanying illustrations are reproduced by express permission of the Society, and by the kindness of Mr. Emery Walker, F.S.A., to whom the photographic negatives belong.

how very easily the various garments fall. The veil over the head, the flowing mantle, and the delicate folds of the gown all indicate that thin and probably rich materials were at this time used in making garments for ladies' wear.

The style and shape of the armour and ornaments worn by Sir John Creke are certainly not less refined. It is an admirable instance of the cyclas period of armour, and closely resembles in type the effigy to the second Sir John d'Aubernoun.

CHAPTER VI

FIFTEENTH CENTURY COSTUME

IN some respects there was little change in the costume of the fourteenth and fifteenth centuries in England. Now, as heretofore, social status or rank and age were indicated by greater length of garments.

The chief advance in fashion is to be found, as might be expected, amongst the wealthier classes, and towards the end of the century. Perhaps the chief change observable in the costume of the time is the opening out of the front of the surcoat, the result being that the doublet beneath is shown.

The mantle was worn fastened over the right shoulder, as may be seen in the effigy (here shown) of Richard Martyn, 1402, which is taken from a monumental brass at Dartford. The special point of interest is that he is shown wearing the mantle fastened by three buttons over the right shoulder. This is an instance of the mantle being worn as part of the ordinary

Richard Martyn, 1402. Civilian wearing the mantle fastened over the right shoulder (Dartford, Kent)

53

costume of a wealthy man, and it is worthy of
note that this was one of the characteristics of the
costume of quite the early part of the fifteenth
century.

An important picture, from the point of view of
costume, is the portrait of Margaret of York, third
wife of Charles the Bold of Burgundy and sister of
King Edward IV of England, which belongs to the
Society of Antiquaries of London. Margaret was the
daughter of Richard Duke of York, and Cecily Nevile,
daughter of the Earl of Westmorland. She married
the last Duke of Burgundy of the French line in
1468, and the picture is believed to have been painted
about that period. The figure, which is life-size,
includes only the head and shoulders of the lady.
On her head is a tall, pointed, black head-dress, which
is partly covered by a gauze veil, one end of which falls
on to the right shoulder. The lady's hair is entirely
concealed by this head-dress.

The dress is composed of a material, possibly
velvet, of orange-red colour, and has a brown edging
following the horizontally-cut front across the bosom.
Round the neck is a rich broad band or collar of
gold, ornamented at regular intervals by rows of
pearls arranged in double and triple rows. From
this collar a large jewel is suspended on the
breast. A gold chain composed of large oblong
links also hangs round the neck. There are no ear-
rings.

The picture, which is in every way a remarkable
piece of work, is believed to have been painted by

PART OF EFFIGY OF SIR JOHN CHYDIOKE, CIRCA 1450. CHRISTCHURCH,
HAMPSHIRE

HEAD OF EFFIGY OF JOHN BEAUFORT, DUKE OF SOMERSET. DIED 1444,
IN WIMBORNE MINSTER, DORSET

Hugo van der Goes, a Flemish artist, born at Ghent, who appears to have been employed upon the public decorations for Margaret's wedding.

The monumental brasses and other sepulchral effigies, which illustrate the costume of this period, are at once numerous and of great importance on account of their accuracy, especially in matters of detail.   Other most useful sources of information on the subject are to be found in illuminated MSS. and mural paintings.

Robert Skern, 1437.
Civilian's costume

Effigies in the round, such as those of Sir John Chydioke, 1455, at Christchurch, Hampshire, and John Beaufort, Duke of Somerset (d. 1444), at Wimborne Minster, Dorset, are admirable examples of the costume of the period ; and many others exist in different English churches.

One of the disappointments about all these archæological "documents," however, is that they afford little, if any, clue as to the materials employed in the costume, and only partially so as to colour.

It is fortunate, therefore, that the written records of the clothes of the period, preserved in wills and inventories, give us precisely the knowledge we require on these two points.

Some important information is contained in the wills of the first half of the fifteenth century. Not only are the garments themselves referred to in precise terms so as to clearly indicate the particular ones intended, but the fact that they are referred to at all in the testamentary documents as individual pieces of clothing is significant, and affords a clear indication of the great value placed upon them.

The following are some noteworthy bequests of clothing, arranged under the date of probate, extracted from wills in the Court of Probate, London:—

1410. Robert Aueray leaves "to William Begelon a grene Gowne and a hoyd percyd wyth Ray, of the Cordy-wynerys leveray."

1418. Thomas Tuoky, esquire, bequeathed " a gown of blew worsted furred wit protes and polles of Martrons ; Also a gowne of gray russet furred with Ionetis and wylde Catis ; also a gowne of grene frese, in ward, &c., and furred with blak Lambe ; also in ward, &c., a furre of bever and oter medled ; also a Hewk of grene and other melly parted ; also a Doubeled of defence covered with red lether ; . . . also a Cloke of Blake russet ; Also a Dobelet covered with Blak gote Lether."

1417–1418. Stephen Thomas, of Lee, Essex, in a codicil drawn up at Rouen, bequeathed "my Russet gowen that I wered and my blac houd, and a nold [an old] bassenet."

1419–1420. John Rogerysson, of London, bequeathed "to the same Roberd my Blewe gowne and my hode of Rede and Blak ; And to Thomas Pykot my whit Ray

gowne, and my rede Hode ; . . . And to William Pert-
nale, A payre schetis and a red doblet, and a keverlet of
Blewe ; . . . And to Thomas Pertenall a peyre of shetis,
and a dagger, and a Bowe with-owte pecis, and a payre
hosen of grene."

1422. Lady Peryne Clanbowe. This testator left many
specific gifts of books, vestments and plate, and the following garments : "a girdell of peerles" "to Iankyn
Myles, my servaunt xxli., and myn eche daies gowne of
marterount." Also to Sir Iohan Coyle "one pare bedes
of corall" to Elizabeth Ioye . . . "and one gown furred
with gret menyvere." To Ionet Oxbourn . . . "and a
gown furred with Cristy gray." To the wife of Iankyn
Miles "a gown furred with Besshe."

1424-1425. Roger Flore (or Flower), esquire, of London,
and Oakham, Rutlandshire. Amongst other bequests were :
"I wul that my gownes for my body, the which ben ffurred
whith pelure, be dalt amongis my childre, to ilke after here
degre and age. . . . And I wul that the remenaunt of my
clothes for my body be dalt amonges my servauntes. And
I wul that Anneys Samon, my wyfes moder, Margaret
Spriggy, and Alys Rowele and Ionet Humberstone, Beatrice
Swetenham, my aunte, and my cosin Sithynge, half ilk of
hem a gode goldringe, or a broche of gold, or a good peyr
of bedys, for a remembraunce of me. And I wil the Maister
of Manton half my pair of bedys that I use my self, with the
ten aves of silver, and a pater noster over-gilt, preying him
to have mynde of me sumtime whan he seith our lady sawter
on hem."

1431-32. Isabel Gregory, of Hackney. "To Ione my
dowter, a blew goune and a grene kyrtyll, and a schete."
"To Ionet Selvester a blake cote, furryd, allso I be-quethe
to Thomas Formannis wyf a russet goune lynyt with whythe
blanket, also to Idany Hale a cloke and a gounne of russet,
furrit."

1433. John Barnet, draper, of London.   "My sanguyn goune to be sold and do for my soule."

1434.   Margarete Asshcombe, widow, of London.   " I bequethe to the wyf of William Hoton my cosyn, a ryng of gold with a crucifix aboune, also y be-quethe to Clemens, the woman that kepes me, a gowne of Musterdevylers and a kyrtell of musterdevylers with grene sleves, and an hode of blak of lure, and an hod of blewe."

1436.   Richard Bokeland, esquire, of All Hallows the Great, Thames Street, London.   " Allso I wol that Thomas Rothewell have myn Prymour and myn purple goune furred with martrons.   Allso I wol that Iohn Melbourne have my scarlet goune furred with martrouns."

1438.   Richard Dixton, esquire, of Cirencester, Gloustershire.

" Item to John Mody a gowne of grene Damaske lyned, and a nother gowne of Russet furred with blak."

1442.   John Wynter, esquire.   " Also to Herry Perreur a new gowne of Russet furred with blak lambe . . . and a lyned gowne of russet of my maistre Fastolf liverey."

In the will of Joan Candell,[1] 1479, we find bequeathed,

To Isabell Hyndeley my best kirtill of violet.   To Elizabeth Wasselyn a gown of the colour of blak.   To Elizabeth Forman a halling (hanging for walls of the hall) of grene, etc.   To Janet Gumby a single gown of murray, etc.

The will of Isabel Grimston,[2] of Flynton, 1479, bequeaths,

To my daughter, Elis Grymston, my furd gown, a rede girdill harnest with silver and gilted, my blak girdill silver

---

[1] *Testamenta Eboracensia,* Vol. III, p. 246.
[2] *Op. cit.,* Vol. III, p. 253.

EFFIGIES OF SIR THOMAS ARDERNE (CIRCA 1400), AND
MATILDA, HIS WIFE, IN ELFORD CHURCH,
STAFFORDSHIRE

harnest, and the half of corall bedis, a gold ryng, and a
purs of cloth of gold.   I wyt to my daughter, Elis Colynson,
my grene gown, a musterdevelis gown with a velwyt colar,
my cremesyn kirtill, half of my corall bedes, a pair of gelt
bedes gawded w^t silver, my blew girdill, and my rede girdill,
a gold ryng, and a purs of Royn.

In the volume of Kentish wills entitled *Testamenta
Cantiana*, published by the Kent Archæological Society,
there are some important entries referring to articles of
costume bequeathed to particular persons, or for particular purposes.   Thus, although money was sometimes left, as, for example,

To the Wardens of the brotherhede of Our Lady in West
Malling towards the sustentation of the brotherhod v marcs
so that they cause my name to be enscribed in thaire bede-
rolle oon the awter there (John Browne, yeoman, 1488);

another method of ensuring commemoration after
death was by means of gifts of rich garments and
costly household articles such as coverlets, which in
the fifteenth and sixteenth centuries were composed of
sumptuous materials.

Thus, in 1529, William Borough, vicar, left to his
church,

My spones of silver to make a paire of cruetts.   Two of
my best coverletts, the oon to hang behynde the sepulchre
and the other afore the high awter.

Sysley Jhonson, wydow, of Dartford, bequeathed, To the
hight aulter my best kercher to make a corporas clothe.

Perse Kyrfote, in 1508, bequeathed to the parish church
of Greenwich a counterpoynte w^t verdors to ly be for the
high aulter on principall festis in the honor of the sacrament

so y^t my wyff have the kepyng y^r of during hir lyff berying hit to ye chirch in the said fests.

Isabella Longeman, widow, in 1521, bequeathed to the church of Allhallows, Hoo,

The coverlet that lieth over me when I am borne to churche.

SUMPTUARY LAWS

The Statutes of the Realm of England contain many most interesting Acts which were passed with a view to regulating the wearing of expensive and fine garments and personal ornaments.

In the eleventh year of Edward II (1337–1338), for example, an Act was brought into force providing that no one should wear fur upon his clothes, excepting the royalty, nobility, "and people of Holy Church" who spent at least a hundred pounds a year of their benefice. The penalty imposed on those of lower position who wore fur was forfeiture of the prohibited article, and such further punishment as the King might see fit to direct.

An Act of the thirty-seventh year of Edward III (1363–1364) made it unlawful for handicraftsmen and yeomen to wear clothes of a higher value than forty shillings the whole cloth; and cloth of silk, cloth of silver, girdles, rings, garters, ouches, ribbands and chains, and other articles of gold were also prohibited.

King Edward IV, in the third year of his reign (1463–1464), Chapter V, passed an Act dealing with the wearing of excessive apparel, and prohibiting it on the ground that it was "to the great Displeasure of God,

ARDERNE TOMB (SOUTH SIDE), ELFORD CHURCH, STAFFORDSHIRE

and impoverishing of this Realm." Cloth of gold, "corses wrought with Gold," and "Furr of Sables," were prohibited for any knight under the estate of a lord. Penalty, forfeiture, and fine of twenty pounds to be paid to the King.

Cloth of velvet upon velvet was not permitted in the case of a knight and his lady unless he were a Knight of the Garter. None lower than a lord was allowed to wear cloth of silk of purple colour. All below the degree of a knight were prohibited from wearing velvet, branched satin, counterfeit cloth of silk, fur of ermine, and imitation velvet.

To the above regulations there were the usual exceptions in favour of members of the royal household, etc.

The Act further provides for the wearing of official costumes by members of corporations, mayors, aldermen, recorders, and the like. Aldermen and their wives were permitted to wear the same quality of garments as was worn by esquires and gentlemen.

"Furr of Martrons, Letuse (pure gray or pure myniver)" were not allowed to be worn by persons possessed of an income of less than forty pounds a year; and those who possessed less than forty shillings a year were not at liberty to clothe themselves in garments made of fustian, bustian, fustian of Naples, scarlet cloth in Grain and fur, black and white lambs' fur excepted.

There were some curious provisions in this Act which were clearly intended to give a monopoly of the newest fashion to the wealthy. Thus, a yeoman was not allowed to use or "wear in Array for his Body, any Bolsters nor stuffing of Wool, Cotton, nor Cadas, nor any stuffing in his Doublet, but only Lining according to the same.

Again, the length of gowns, jackets, and cloaks was the subject of precise regulations. Thus no knight under the estate of a lord, no esquire, nor gentleman, nor any other person, was permitted to wear a gown, jacket, or coat unless it was long enough to cover the upper part of the thigh. Servants in husbandry, labourers, etc., were not allowed to array themselves in cloth if the price thereof exceeded two shillings the broad yard.

In the twenty-second year of Edward IV (1482–1483), Cap. I, the regulations touching apparel were made more stringent. Cloth of gold and silk of purple colour were prohibited to all except the King, the Queen, the King's mother, the King's children, and the King's brothers and sisters. No one under the estate of a duke might wear gold of tissue, and no man lower than a lord might wear plain cloth of gold. Doublets or gowns trimmed with velvet were limited to those of or above the rank of knight; and damask or "satten" in the gown were limited to esquires of the King's body. Damask, sateen, and gowns of chamlet were reserved for those who were of the degree of esquires or gentlemen.

In the first year of Henry VIII's reign (1509–1510), "An Act agaynst wearing of costly Apparrell" was passed, in which the use of cloth of gold of purple colour and purple silk was restricted to the King and his immediate family, and similar regulations to those of Edward IV above referred to were made as to the wearing of velvets, furs, and other costly materials. Foreign "woollen cloth" and foreign furs were prohibited to certain ranks, and the length of cloth employed in long gowns, riding gowns, etc., became the subject of limitations.

In the sixth year of Henry VIII (1514-1515), another "Acte of Apparell" was passed in which much the same regulations were laid down.

In the following year, the seventh of Henry VIII (1515-1516), a longer statute was made, of which the following is a quotation to show the precise regulations laid down, the latter part of the Act being summarized for the sake of brevity and unnecessary repetition of legal formulæ.

THACTE OF APPARELL

Forasmoche as the grette and costeley arrey and apparell usid wythin this realme, contarye to good statute thereof made, hath ben the occasyon of grette impoverysshyng of dyvers of the King's Subjects and provokyd dyvers of them to robbe and to do extorcyon and other unlaufull dedys to maynteyn theirby their costeley arrey ; In eschewyng wherof be it ordeynd by thauctorite of thys present parliament that no person of what estate condycion or degre that he be, use in his apparell any cloth of gold of p^{r}poure colour, or sylke of p^{r}poure colour or furr called furre of blak geynetts, but only the King the Quene, the Kyngs moder the Kings Chyldren, the Kyngs Brethern and Susters [upon payn to forfeit the said apparell wherwith soever] ytt be myxte and for using the same to forfeit for every tyme so [offending xx. li.   And that no Man other than the Kings Children] under the estate of a Duke or Marques use in any apparell of his [body or upon his horses or hors harnes any cloth of Gold of] Tyssue uppon (pain?) of forfeyture of the same apparell wherwyth soever ytt be myxte [garded or browderd out that for using the same to forfett for every] tyme so offendyng xx marcs ;

And that no man other than the [Kings Children or undre the] degre of a Duke or Duks son and heir apparaunt Marques or Erle, use or were in hys apparell any furre of Sables, uppon payne to forfeyte the same apparell and for using the same to forfayte for every tyme so offendyng xx marcs. And that no man under the degre of a Son of a Duke, Marques or Erle, and the Sonnes and Heirs apparaunt of and under the degre of a Baron, use in hys apparell of hys body or hys horse or horseharneys any cloth of gold or cloth of sylver, ne any suche apparell myxte garded and imbrowderd wyth gold or sylver, uppon payn of forfeyture of the same apparell and for using the same to forfeytte for every tyme so offending x marcs ; And that no man, under the degre of the son of a Duke Erle or the Degre of a Baron or a Knyght of the Garter, were any wollen clothe made oute of this realme of England Ireland Walys Calyce or the marches of the same or Barwyke except only in bonetts, uppon payne of forfeiture of the seid cloth, except before except, and for usyng the same to forfette for every tyme so offending x marcs. And that no man, under the degre of a Knyght of the Garter were in hys gowne or cote or any other hys apparell of hys body, or apparell of hys horse, any velvett of the colour of cremesyn or blewe uppon payn to forfette the same apparell and for usyng the same to forfayte for every time so offendyng xls.

And that no man, under the Degre of the son & heyre apparaunt of a Baron Knyght & Squyers for the Kyngs body hys Cupberers Kervers and Servers havyng the ordynary fee for the same, and the Cupberers Kervers &

Servers for the Quene & the Prynce havyng the ordynarye fee for the same, the Treasourer of the Kyngs chamber and all other Squyers for the Kyngs body Cupberers Kervers & Servers, and others havyng possessyon of lands and tents or other hereditaments in their hands or other to their use to the yerely valour of CC marcs. Justices of the oon benche and of the other, the Maister of the Rolls and Barounys of the Kyngs Exchequyer and all other of the Kyngs Counsell or Quenes Counsell and the Kyngs and the Quenes Phisicions, and the Mayres of the Citie of London for the tyme beyng, use or wear any velvet in their gowns Jaketts nor coots, or furres of Martrens in their apparell; uppon payn to forfette the same furres & apparell wherwyth soever ytt be myxte, joynyd garderd or browderd and for usyng of the same to forfett for every time so offend-yng xls.

Except alwey and provyded that suche other officers & servaunts of the Kyngs most honorabull household and of the Quenes Household and of the Prynce for the tyme beyng, putt in suche romes offics and servycs as hereafter be expressyd may use & wear velvet in their garments and apparell in suche maner and fourme onlye as hereafter ys lymytted & declared in this acte; this present acte or any-thyng conteyned theryn not wythstandyng.

Item ytt ys provyded that no man under the degrees above namyd, except the sonnes & heires apparant of Knyghts and also except gentylmen havyng lands or fees of the yerely valewe of CC marcs over all charges were or use any cheyne or colar of gold or gylte or any gold aboute hys necke nor in their brateletts, uppon payn of forfeyture of the same : Except suche offycers and servaunts of the Kings the Quenes and the Princes most honorabull households as in this acte be expressyd and lycensyd at their pleasure so to do.

Item ytt ys exceptyd and provyded that the sonnes and

F

heirs apparaunts of all persons above namyd may were in their dubletts velvett of blak colour and in their gownes Jaketts and cotes damask of blak Russett & tawny colour and chamlet, wythout offence of this statute.

The Act goes on to provide that no ordinary person shall wear "Saten or Damaske in their gownes Jaketts or cotes"; but a gentleman having a clear annual income of a hundred marks derived from lands, etc., was excepted.

No man under the degree of a gentleman, except graduates of the Universities, yeomen, grooms, pages, and certain officials of the royal household was permitted to wear foreign furs, upon pain of forfeiture of the same and the payment of a fine of forty shillings.

Embroidered garments were prohibited to all beneath the rank of a son of a Knight of the Garter. Similar restrictions were placed upon the quantity of cloth used in a garment and the quality of the article worn, the price even being precisely defined.

No one beneath the degree of a knight, with certain specified exceptions, was allowed to wear "any pynchyd shyrt or pynchyd partlet of lynnyn cloth or playn shyrt garnysshyd or made wyth sylke or gold or sylver," on pain of forfeiture and the payment of a fine of ten shillings.

By an Act of the fifth of Queen Elizabeth (1562-1563), cap. 6, vendors of foreign apparel were not permitted to sell their wares to any one not having an annual income of £3000.

A recent writer[1] on English costume in the Middle

[1] D. J. Medley in *Social England*, Vol. II.

PORTRAIT OF ARTHUR, PRINCE OF WALES, FIRST SON OF HENRY VII.
(BORN 1486. DIED 1502)

Ages draws attention to a point which must be borne in mind in any attempt to get a clear idea of this very fascinating subject.

" It is also necessary to remember," he remarks in speaking of the evidence of inventories, " that mediæval society was far more dominated with the idea of caste than the society with which we are familiar, and that this caste, whether social or merely official, was outwardly marked by a difference of costumes."

This is a fact which is perfectly clear to any one who has made himself familiar with old English costume, and it will afford a useful key to the varieties of the dresses worn by different people.

CHAPTER VII

SIXTEENTH CENTURY COSTUME

THIS century covers a period of great importance in the history of English costume. The magnificence and even extravagance of the Tudors in the matter of dress are well known. Henry VIII and Queen Elizabeth stand out in history as two of the most gorgeously clad sovereigns England has ever known. The vanity that delighted in fine clothes naturally favoured perpetuation in the direction of portraiture, and some of the most valuable sources of information we now possess on the fashions and foibles of the time are to be found in the numerous royal portraits which Holbein and his successors painted.

Perhaps the most noteworthy of all the leaders of English fashion before the eighteenth century was Queen Elizabeth. Her personal vanity, her special love of elaborate and costly dresses, and the enormous wardrobe which she possessed, united to make her, in every sense of the term, the leader of feminine costume during a large part of the sixteenth century.

The portraits of Henry VIII painted by Holbein are not only extraordinarily fine as masterpieces of the portrait painter's art, but are also probably the best

KING HENRY VIII

PORTRAIT OF QUEEN MARY
FROM A DRAWING OF THE ORIGINAL BY LUCAS DE HERE

evidence now in existence for the costume of the most remarkable of our Tudor kings.

The most favoured costume of Henry VIII seems to have been a richly ornamented doublet, sometimes of cloth of gold enriched with jewels, and slashed at frequent intervals in perpendicular lines. Over this was a rich surcoat of crimson material or cloth of gold embroidered with gold and lined with ermine. The cod-piece was prominent and elaborately ornamented. The head-dress was a richly jewelled, flat cap with handsome flowing feather. Chains, rings, and a variety of other jewellery completed the attire, which, in spite of a certain vulgarity and loudness, must be described as magnificent in the extreme, and not out of harmony with the burly form of the wearer. The portraits are usually three-quarter length, but such as show the entire figure (the portrait in Viscount Dillon's collection at Ditchley, for instance) represent the King in close-fitting hose, and square-toed and highly elaborated shoes. A glove is usually carried in one hand.

Fine portraits of Henry VIII, showing him in elaborate and rich attire, exist at St. James's Palace, London; the Royal Collection at Windsor Castle; and Trinity Hall, Cambridge.

The ruff as an article of ladies' costume belongs essentially to the period of Queen Elizabeth, including the period when she was princess as well as the time when she occupied the throne. Mr. F. M. O'Donoghue, F.S.A., points out that the entire history of the rise and progress of this remarkable article of attire may be traced in the portraits of Elizabeth,[1] and, indeed, he founds his classification of those portraits on the form of the ruff. He points out that the first suggestion of the ruff is found in the small frill worn as decorations of the collar by both men and women during the reigns of Henry VIII, Edward VI, and Mary. Elizabeth had not long succeeded to the throne before the ruff began to be worn much larger, and soon it became a very striking feature of costume.

The introduction of the art of clear-starching from Holland, and the use of "poking-sticks" for the arrangement of the folds favoured the growth of ruffs, which quickly increased to an astonishing size.

The ruff appears in various forms and styles, but no regular chronological order or sequence has yet been made out. On the contrary, the different styles seem to have been more or less contemporaneous. They indicate, not a regular series of gradations from one shape to another, but the whim or caprice of each individual wearer.

Generally speaking, the ruff was shaped by arranging the lace and other delicate materials employed in close convolutions or quillings. Sometimes ruffs took the form of a number of radiating pipes. In the earlier stages of the wearing of the ruff, a circular form was persistently worn. Later on one finds a small opening in front, and sometimes the ruff did not entirely enclose the neck, but was attached to the shoulders, and rose high behind the head.

Ruffs were worn by judges in former times, and they

[1] *Catalogue of the Portraits of Queen Elizabeth*, 1894, p. xiv *et seq.*

KING EDWARD VI

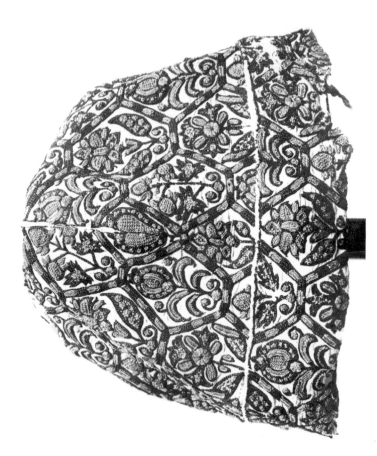

LINEN CAP EMBROIDERED WITH PLAITED SILVER-GILT THREAD AND BLACK SILK

(SECOND HALF OF THE SIXTEENTH CENTURY)

added considerably to the picturesque character of their official robes ; but whilst wigs have survived until the present time, ruffs have long since been discarded.

Among other interesting garments from the Isham Collection, now in the Victoria and Albert Museum, at South Kensington, is a linen cap with broad turned-up edge, embroidered with plaited silver-gilt thread and black silk. The pattern is arranged in a series of somewhat irregular six-sided compartments. The work is believed to be of the second half of the sixteenth century.

The splendid costume of the ladies of England during the latter part of the Tudor period is well represented in the portraits of Queen Mary and Queen Elizabeth. Of the former Queen there is a remarkable portrait by Lucas de Here, evidently painted from the life, in the possession of the Society of Antiquaries of London. Besides being probably the largest signed picture by this artist, this painting is noteworthy as being the best portrait of Mary in the kingdom, being excelled by only one other portrait now in Spain. The Queen, represented as a three-quarter-length figure, is shown standing. On her head she wears the French hood. This interesting head-dress, so fashionable at the period, consists of a dark, probably black, close-fitting cap covering the crown, and leaving the hair uncovered in front. Above it is a second cap or hood with richly jewelled border, befitting the exalted rank of the wearer. The enrichments on the upper part of the hood consist of pearls arranged in groups of fours.

The dress, composed of rich brown material, with bold yellow pattern, fits close to the body and shoulders, and there are large, loose sleeves of dark brown fur falling from a point a little above the elbow in each case. At the neck the dress opens into a widespread collar, displaying a necklace and cross fastened round the neck. On her breast is a handsome enamelled jewel, and a large pearl depending from it. Another beautiful jewel of circular form hangs by a cord from a jewelled girdle round the waist. The skirt of the dress is open in front, disclosing an embroidered kirtle of great beauty. The sleeves are well developed and enriched with numerous stones of square form in gold settings, straps and embroidery somewhat resembling that of the kirtle.

The portrait was painted in 1554, the year of Mary's marriage with Philip of Spain. What gives it its chief interest, perhaps, is that it represents a grand English lady about the middle of the sixteenth century rather than a queen.

Another picture of Queen Mary I, also by Lucas de Here, is in the possession of Sir W. Cuthbert Quilter, Bart. It was recently exhibited at the Royal Academy (Winter Exhibition, 1908, No. 4). She wears in this portrait a salmon- or flesh-coloured gown with embroidered collar of deep brown. Her kirtle, or "fore part," as it is styled in some Elizabethan accounts, is of dark colour, if not quite black; the outer gown, which has a loose, open collar, is of dark brown or reddish hue and is purfled or edged and trimmed with gold lace. Extra sleeves, richly

QUEEN JANE SEYMOUR

trimmed with deep brown fur, adorn the arms, and, generally speaking, closely resemble those in the portrait belonging to the Society of Antiquaries. The head-dress is jewelled and a rare form of the Paris or French hood class.

The portraits of Queen Elizabeth have a special interest and importance for students of costume because of the love of splendour and parade which that Queen's dresses always display. The same reason may also account for the large numbers of contemporary portraits which have survived until our day.

In the Royal Collection at Windsor Castle there is a portrait which shows Elizabeth at the age of about thirteen. It represents her life-size and down to a little below the knees. On her head is a richly-jewelled red French hood. Her dress is also red and is furnished with widely opened outer sleeves, within which are white, gold-embroidered under-sleeves drawn in at the wrists with deep ruffles. The dress is cut somewhat low at the bosom and so wide as to leave shoulders as well as neck bare. The skirt of the dress is open in front and shows a gold-embroidered kirtle beneath. The girdle is jewelled, as also is the upper margin of the dress. There is a handsome jewel on the dress just over the bosom. Another hangs from one of the two necklaces which adorn the neck, whilst others hang from the back of the French hood. The portrait is a charming piece of composition, and although the name of the artist is not known, he is supposed, with good reason, to have been of the French school of Holbein.

Another portrait of Elizabeth in the Royal Collection at Hampton Palace is contained in an allegorical picture with representations of Juno, Venus, and Minerva. The Queen is crowned and bears a sceptre in the right hand, and an orb in the left. Her dress is dark with light sleeves, the skirt open in front showing a kirtle diapered with pearls. The picture was painted by Lucas de Here.

A portrait of Elizabeth uncrowned, and while still young, painted by an artist belonging to the school of M. Gheeraedts, gives some interesting details of costume. Her hair, plainly dressed, is confined in a gold caul studded with pearls. The ruff is edged with gold. The dress is of crimson velvet, cut square at the bosom. The neck is covered with a muslin partlet which is adorned with pearls and gold, and open in front in such a way as to show a pendent jewel. She wears no ear-rings. The picture is undated, but there is an inscription, believed not to be contemporary, to the effect that it represents "the Lady Elizabeth her Picture when she was in the Tower."

Another important portrait of Elizabeth when young is in the National Portrait Gallery. On her head is an arched head-dress of jewels from which gauze veil falls behind. She wears a richly patterned black dress ornamented with a kind of network or lattice-work of gold cords and pearls, with white puffings on the shoulders and bodice. The dress is cut low and square at the bosom, the neck being partially covered with a white network ornamented with a black pattern. An enamelled badge representing a phœnix rising from

Queen Elizabeth, as Princess, in 1554
(From a painted panel discovered at Little Gaddesden, Herts)

flames (one of Elizabeth's devices) is suspended from her shoulders by a richly jewelled collar, in the centre of which is a large rose with diamond in the middle. Part of a feather fan which Elizabeth holds is visible in the picture.

The following are brief details of some of the costumes in which Elizabeth appears in other portraits. In all of these she is represented wearing a small frill-ruff.

Cobham Hall (Earl of Darnley).—Low head-dress adorned with pearls, and grey veil falling behind. White, high-necked dress, the bodice buttoned and frogged down the front, and the sleeves and skirt patterned with a design in yellow.

Great Hampden (Earl of Buckinghamshire).—Low head-dress. Dress with high collar, and close-fitting mahoitered sleeves, and small ruffles at the wrists.

University Library, Cambridge.—Jewelled head-dress, with gauze veil, edged with spangles, falling over the shoulders. The dress is cut low at the bosom, and the neck covered with a white and gold partlet.

Madresfield Court (Earl Beauchamp).—Head-dress formed of white puffings, with gauze veil, crossed with lines of gold. Black dress with broad band of gold brocade down the front. The sleeves are white, worked with flowers, and have lace ruffles and gauze over-sleeves. Pearl necklaces, girdle of jewels, and one ring.

Holyrood Palace (His Majesty the King).—Flowers and pearls in hair. Close-fitting black dress, with grey opaque muslin mantle, which is wired out behind, and passes over the upper part of both arms. Ruffles at the wrists. Double necklace of small pearls is looped up to the right breast, and an enamelled jewel is on the left breast. Girdle of jewels and pearls.

Ashridge (Earl Brownlow).— High-crowned black hat and red dress, which is open at the neck and down the front of the shirt, displaying a white kirtle.

Hampton Court Palace (Royal Collection).—Head-dress of red silk trimmed with pearls; a thick veil also adorned with pearls, and white satin puffs falling over the shoulders. White dress, slashed and studded with pearls, is high at the neck, with a jewelled collar. Ruffles at the wrists.

National Portrait Gallery.—White satin dress with narrow slashes and gold bands, studded with red and black square jewels set in gold, and brown veil which is gathered up in plaits over the head and studded with pearls. Elizabeth is here shown in somewhat advanced age.

Henham Hall (Earl of Stradbroke).—Similar to the above.

Lord Rothschild's Collection.—High-necked black dress with pointed stomacher and white mahoitered sleeves, which are decorated with ball-like flowers of gauze and rows of pearls, and veil with wired-out bowed wings, edged with pearls. Large diamond with three pearls pendent from it on the bosom, with a pelican " in piety " in gold above it, two long chains of pearls and jewels and jewelled girdle.

Sudeley Castle (Mrs. Dent).—Elizabeth wears a small head-dress, small quilled ruff, high-necked dress, and long girdle.

PROCESSION OF QUEEN ELIZABETH

Lord Kenyon's Collection.—Elizabeth as Princess. She wears a jewelled head-dress, small, close-fitting frill-like ruff, edged with gold, ruffles at the wrists to match, fur-trimmed black dress cut low at the bosom, partlet of white material and gold, having a small opening in front showing a gold necklace with a black ring suspended, tight mahoitered sleeves slashed and embroidered, and jewelled girdle.

Overton Hall.—Life-size picture, showing Elizabeth wearing low, jewelled head-dress with white veil falling from it, thick quilled ruff, high-necked white dress, the bodice and sleeves of which are slashed and decorated with stripes of gold, and sleeveless black surcoat trimmed with gold brocade. The ruffles at the wrists match the ruff. Her jewellery includes a rich carcanet, with large jewel hanging on the breast, a jewelled girdle, and rings on both hands.

The following are a few particulars of portraits in which Elizabeth is wearing a radiating and unbroken ruff :—

Wimpole (Earl of Hardwicke).—She wears a large jewelled head-dress surmounted by an arched crown, and with falling veil which has large, lace-edged, wired-out wings ; large quilled ruff, with short pearl necklace above it ; and another necklace of pearls descending to the waist. The skirt of the dress is patterned with eyes and ears, and on the sleeve is embroidered a serpent. At the wrists are lace ruffles.

National Portrait Gallery.—Elizabeth in this picture is represented crowned with a small jewelled crown, and wearing a black outer dress garnished with red

bows and opened in front, showing white kirtle below
it.   The sleeves are full and drawn in at the wrists.
The grey lace ruff is interesting, being formed of flat
pieces overlapping one another like the sections of a
fan, and there is also a smaller ruff inside, fitting close
to the face.

Woburn Abbey.—In a picture belonging to the Duke
of Bedford at Woburn Abbey, and commemorating
the Spanish Armada, the Queen is shown wearing a
black head-dress adorned with feathers and jewels;
a large, high-rising ruff fitting close under the chin;
a stomacher and the skirt of outer dress, both of white
satin and jewelled; sleeves and under-skirt black,
and trimmed with pearls and jewelled bows; and full
sleeves drawn in at the wrists with lace cuffs.

Hatfield House.—There is a picture here in which
the Queen is wearing a large head-dress edged with
standing-up jewelled ornaments and rich ruff, fitting
close under the chin, with winged gauze veil falling
behind.   The dress is black, the stomacher covered
with rows of pearls and other jewels, and she has rich
lace cuffs.

Saltram (Earl of Morley).—The chief point of interest
about this portrait is that the Queen has jewels in her
hair, a large pearl on the forehead, and a chain of
pearls, garnished with white satin bows, suspended
from her shoulders.

Charlecote Park (Miss Lucy).—In this portrait Elizabeth wears a crown-like head-dress of pearls, and black
dress decorated with gold and jewels.   The skirt,
open in front, shows a white kirtle ornamented with

MARGARET, DUCHESS OF NORFOLK

(DIED 1563, AGED 23.) SHE WAS THE SECOND WIFE OF THOMAS, FOURTH DUKE OF NORFOLK

a pattern in gold. The stomacher is pointed; the sleeves are large cuffs of rich lace. The ruff does not fit close, but shows the neck, with a collar of pearls, above it.

The Weavers' Company.—Elizabeth in this portrait wears a head-dress with falling veil, which partly covers the left arm; black dress, the bodice of which is decorated with festoons of pearls, and having large open sleeves, and under-sleeves richly embroidered with flowers; and there are lace ruffles at the wrists. The grey lace ruff is of the "piped" variety, and a pearl necklace is seen above it.

Christ Church, Oxford.—The dress in this case is of a dark brown colour, the stomacher and outer skirt being jewelled. The sleeves are puffed and jewelled, with lace ruffles at the wrists. The skirt is open in front, showing white kirtle. The piped ruff is large and of geometrical pattern. There is a pearl necklace above it which descends to the waist.

Penshurst Place.—Elizabeth wears a tiara-like head-dress, jewelled and quilled, with thick, white, pearl-studded veil falling from it over the shoulders. A thick, narrow quilled ruff fits close under the chin. The dress is black, embroidered and jewelled down the front, and cut low and square at the bosom. The neck is covered with a jewelled gauze partlet. The outer sleeves are full and of gauze. The under-sleeves are close-fitting and of white material, patterned with black and covered with jewels. There are lace ruffles at the wrists, and the Queen wears a pearl necklace and girdle.

G

Powerscourt Castle.—Jewelled head-dress from which falls a veil ; green dress with white sleeves and partlet, which are ornamented with flower pattern, and quilled ruffles at the wrists. A pearl necklace is festooned on her breast, and a girdle of pearls and jewels encircles her waist.

Welbeck Abbey.—The costume consists of a large head-dress of jewels and pearls ; rich lace piped ruff, fitting close to the chin ; white dress patterned with flowers ; and a dark mantle adorned with roses which descends to the ground behind ; a jewelled collar with pendent badge hanging from the shoulders ; and a pearl necklace reaching to the waist.

Lord Hothfield's Collection.—This is a life-size bust of the Queen showing a head-dress of pearls and red stones ; a red rose near the left ear ; piped chin ruff ; white dress decorated with gold fleur-de-lis, with large diamonds and red stones at the shoulders ; and necklaces of large pearls, diamonds, and rubies over the breast.

Longford Castle.—This is a remarkable portrait painted late in the Queen's life. The costume comprises arched head-dress of jewels and white puffs, plain quilled chin ruff dentelled at the edges, and high-necked black dress decorated with pearls arranged in groups of four.

Petworth (Robert Downing, Esq.).—Another portrait of Elizabeth late in life. The main features of the costume are low, jewelled head-dress, with pearl hanging on the forehead ; high-necked black dress with close-fitting white sleeves patterned with black flowers and studded with jewels ; large gauze outer sleeves ;

broad band of gold brocade, adorned with jewels, down
the front of the dress; girdle of pearls and jewels
encircling the waist; and ruffles and long lace cuffs at
the wrists.

Hampton Court (Royal Collection).—Portrait of the
Queen in old age. The head-dress of white satin and
jewels is tiara-like, and has a gauze veil falling from it
behind; rich quilled ruff fitting close under the chin;
black bodice; white sleeves patterned with black
flowers; lace ruffles at the wrists; large pearl in the
ear; and three necklaces of pearls falling over the
breast.

Corsham (Lord Methuen). — Life-size portrait of
Elizabeth wearing an outer robe bordered with ermine,
which is open in front and has hanging sleeves. The
stomacher and sleeves of the under-dress are enriched
with jewels. The hair is also decorated with jewels,
and a pearl hangs from her forehead. The dress is
high at the neck, and the escalloped ruff fits close
under the chin.

The following are a few details of pictures of Queen
Elizabeth in which she is represented as wearing a
radiating ruff, open in front.

The Trinity House, Tower Hill.—On the head is an
arched crown of pearls and a veil with wired-out gauze
wings.

Jesus College, Oxford.—The Queen wears an open,
arched crown; a rich piped lace ruff; lace-edged veil,
with wired-out gauze wings; bodice of dress cut low
and square, and patterned with pearls and jewels; an

enamelled device with figure of Diana attached to the left sleeve, and a figure of a knight on horseback attached to the right one ; short necklace, with red pendent jewel ; and jewelled hair.

Trinity College, Cambridge.—Brocaded dress cut low and square, with long pointed stomacher, deep lace cuffs, and open, hanging outer sleeves ; white feather and large pearls in the hair. From the end of the stomacher descends a pink ribbon which is looped up to a circular jewel with pendent pearl.

Boughton House, Northants (Duke of Buccleuch).— This represents Elizabeth at the age of 61 (1594). The Queen wears a white dress with long pointed stomacher and large farthingale. The stomacher is richly jewelled ; the skirt patterned with a geometrical design and studded with pearls, and the sleeves ornamented with lines of puffings, divided by jewels. No head-dress, but there are several jewels in the hair, and three large pearls hang on the forehead. A close-fitting necklace of five rows of pearls is seen through the opening in front of her high-rising, rich piped lace ruff. Deep lace cuffs at the wrists.

Condover Hall.—A portrait of the Queen in old age. She is wearing a black cap, high-rising piped lace ruff, close-fitting pearl necklace, and red dress. The stomacher is of white satin edged with pearls, and full sleeves patterned with arabesques.

Gorhambury.—In this portrait the Queen wears a close black head-dress and large quilled ruff, above which is a pearl necklace descending in three ropes down the centre and sides of the stomacher. The whole dress is chequered black and gold, with small lace cuffs.

Representations of Queen Elizabeth with high ruff, open in front, exist in several collections. The following are brief particulars of some of the most important :—

National Portrait Gallery.—The Queen wears a small jewelled crown. Her dress is richly ornamented, and a rope of pearls hangs from her neck down to the waist.

Rousham Hall.—Dress consists of crimson velvet robes with ermine mantle and farthingale. A loop of pearls hangs from the right side of the Queen's waist, and on each side of the ruff is a jewel.

Hardwick Hall.—In this picture the Queen wears a jewelled ruff; veil with wired-out gauze wings edged with pearls; black dress studded with pearls, sleeves puffed and jewelled; and white kirtle ornamented with animals, monsters, and flowers. The body of the dress is cut low and square. At the wrists are lace cuffs covered with diamonds. She also wears a long pointed stomacher and farthingale, the latter being decorated with a large jewel, white shoes studded with diamonds, two necklaces, pearl ear-drop, and jewels in the hair.

Fryston Hall (Lord Houghton). — Small arched crown formed of pearls; rich bone-lace ruff and cuffs; gauze veil with wired-out wings, black ermine-lined mantle open in front showing red gown beneath; pearl necklace and ear-rings; also the collar of St. George and the sceptre.

Parham Park (Lord Zouch).—Blue head-dress surmounted by a crown of pearls; large ruff of very rich blue lace; veil with wired-out wings edged with pearls; yellow-brown dress decorated with a large leaf pattern; and pointed stomacher and large farthingale. She also wears numerous jewels.

Maison Dieu, Dover.—Arched crown of pearls; ermine-lined mantle; large lace ruff; crimson dress, with long stomacher and large farthingale; lace cuffs and chains of pearls at the wrists; numerous diamonds, pearls, and other jewels.

St. James's Palace, London (Royal Collection).—Head-dress formed of gauze flowers with wire stalks on which are pearls; low-necked black dress, the upper part of which is sown with pearls, and the satin skirt adorned with velvet quatrefoils, pearls, etc.

Hatfield House (the Marquess of Salisbury).—High head-dress, plumed and jewelled; a flowered dress cut low and square at the bosom; loose outer robe, with open, hanging sleeves; gauze veil, with large, wired-out wings edged with pearls; wide ruff, with small, close-fitting frill round the neck, and similar frills at the wrists; also rubies, pearls, an enamelled jewel, etc.

Sherborne Castle.—This fine picture represents Queen Elizabeth seated in a litter and carried by six noblemen, surrounded by courtiers. The Queen wears a high-peaked head-dress; low-necked white dress entirely covered with puffings and studded with jewels, with close-fitting sleeves and lace cuffs; and wide-spreading ruff with small, close-fitting inner frill. She also has several jewels in the hair, etc.

QUEEN ELIZABETH
(PAINTER UNKNOWN)

Bodleian Library, Oxford. — In this portrait the Queen wears a white dress the sleeves and stomacher of which are decorated with a yellow and red pattern.

Ditchley (Viscount Dillon).—This noble portrait represents Elizabeth at the age of fifty-nine. She is represented as standing on a map of England, and wearing a high-peaked head-dress; low-necked dress entirely white, with white puffings, and studded with jewels; large, wired-out gauze wings edged with jewels; hanging outer sleeves which reach to the ground; long pointed stomacher, and farthingale. She has also a short necklace with a rich pendent jewel, another long necklace passes down over the bosom, a rope of pearls falls from the shoulders to the waist, and an ear-drop is attached by a scarlet ribbon near the left ear.

At *Burghley House* (Marquess of Exeter) and at *Knole*, Kent, there are inferior copies of this picture, the former being only a bust.

The Grove, Watford (Earl of Clarendon). — This picture represents Elizabeth wearing a high black gown with large gold buttons from the neck down to the waist. The gown is trimmed with lace on the sleeves, round the wrists, upon the shoulders, and round the top. The Queen wears a single row of pearls round the neck, and a triple row hanging down to the waist.

The remarkable portraits of Queen Elizabeth in fancy dress at Hatfield House and Hampton Court Palace, although important as historical pictures and

as works of art, are of small value as illustrations of
the actual costumes of the period in which they were
painted.

Major Holford possesses a superb portrait of the
first Lord Delaware, which was recently exhibited at
the Royal Academy (Winter Exhibition, 1908, No. 2).
The picture is of the highest excellence as a work
of art, and is possibly of even more value as an illustration of the costume of a gentleman of high rank
in the latter half of the sixteenth century.

The shirt is of embroidered, light-coloured satin, and,
although little of it shows, enough is visible to expose
the cord fastenings by which it was tied at the neck.
The outer cloak, the jacket or tunic, trunks, nether hose,
and cap are all of black colour, some of them being
slashed, or rather decorated, with pullings-out of
crimson.   The black cap is most interesting, being
decorated with a white plume, whilst its whole surface
is powdered with jewels alternately triangular and circular in form.   Lord Delaware died in the year 1595,
which was a considerably later date, probably, than
that of the portrait.   William Stretes, the painter
of this fine picture, was painter to Edward VI in 1551,
and is known to have executed a famous portrait of
the Earl of Surrey dated 1547.   This portrait of Lord
Delaware may, perhaps, have been painted in or about
the year 1550.

An admirable description of the wardrobe of a lady
about the middle of Elizabeth's reign is contained
in a song entitled *A new courtly sonnet of the Lady*

THOMAS HOWARD, FOURTH DUKE OF NORFOLK. (BEHEADED 1572)

Greensleves, and published in 1584. The following
lines give the more important details :—

> I bought thee kerchers to thy head,
>   That were wrought fine and gallantly :
> I kept them, both at board and bed,
>   Which cost my purse well-favour'dly.
>
> I bought thee petticoats of the best,
>   The cloth so fine as fine might be :
> I gave thee jewels for thy chest ;
>   And all this cost I spent on thee.
>
> Thy smock of silk both fair and white,
>   With gold embroider'd gorgeously :
> Thy petticoat of sendall right ;
>   And this I bought thee gladly.
>
> Thy girdle of gold so red,
>   With pearls bedecked sumptuously,
> Unlike no other lasses had :
>   And yet thou wouldest not love me !
>
> Thy purse, and eke thy gay gilt knives,
>   Thy pin-case, gallant to the eye :
> No better wore the burgess' wives :
>   And yet thou wouldest not love me !
>
> Thy crimson stockings, all of silk,
>   With gold all wrought above the knee ;
> Thy pumps, as white as was the milk :
>   And yet thou wouldest not love me.
>
> Thy gown was of the grassy green,
>   Thy sleeves of satin hanging by ;
> Which made thee be our harvest queen :
>   And yet thou wouldest not love me !

> Thy garters fringed with the gold,
> And silver aglets hanging by ;
> Which made thee blithe for to behold :
> And yet thou wouldest not love me !

Some of the varieties of caps worn during the reign of Queen Elizabeth are mentioned in *The Ballad of the Caps*, a poetic effusion of the sixteenth century, of which the following are a few extracts :—

> The Monmouth-cap, the saylors thrum,
> And that wherein the tradesmen come,
> The physic, lawe, the cap divine,
> The same that crowns the muses nine,
> The cap that fools do countenance,
> The goodly cap of maintenance,
>   And any cap, whate're it bee
>   Is still the sign of some degree.

> The sickly cap, both plain and wrought,
> The fuddling-cap, however bought ;
> The quilted, furr'd, the velvet, satin,
> For which so many pates learn latin.
> The crewell cap, the fustian pate,
> The perriwig, the cap of late
>   And any cap, whate're it bee
>   Is still the sign of some degree.

The following extract from Heywood's *Rape of Lucrece*, a sixteenth century composition, is an interesting commentary on the popular costume of the time :—

> O ye fine sunny country lasses,
> That would for brooks change crystal glasses,
> And be transhap'd from foot to crown,
> And straw beds change for beds of down ;

Your partlets turn into nebatoes,
And stead of carrots eat potatoes ;
Your frontlets lay by, and your rails
And fringe with gold your draggl'd tails.
Now your hawk-noses shall have hoods
And billements with golden studs :
Straw hats shall be no more bongraces,
From the bright sun to hide your faces,
For hempen smocks to help the itch,
Have linen sewed with silver stitch ;
And wheresoe'er they chance to stride
One bare before to be their guide.

CHAPTER VIII

SEVENTEENTH CENTURY COSTUME

THE story of English costume during the reign of James I is practically a continuation of that of the latter part of Elizabeth's reign. James I favoured the wearing of quilted and stuffed doublets and breeches, and thus set the fashion in this direction. Towards the end of his reign, however, short jackets, or doublets, with tabs and false sleeves hanging behind, took the place of the long-waisted doublets. The hose, too, instead of being slashed or laced, were covered with loose, broad straps richly adorned with buttons or embroidery, the silk or velvet trunks being visible at the intervals.

Two effigies on the tomb of Sir Richard Baker in Canterbury Cathedral give excellent illustrations of the costume worn by a lady and gentleman at the beginning of this century. The lady, who lies in what has been appropriately called the "toothache" attitude, wears a ruff at the neck and a gown with tightly-fitting bodice and somewhat full skirt, the hips being distended by means of farthingales. The sleeves, which are shaped to the arm, are fastened with six buttons at the wrist, and have turned-back cuffs.

Sir Richard Baker wears a ruff at the neck, small

EFFIGIES OF SIR RICHARD BAKER AND LADY THORNHURST (DIED 1609)
IN CANTERBURY CATHEDRAL

ruffs at the wrists, body- and leg-armour, and padded trunks.

The very last stage in the decadence of armour is represented in the effigy of George Hodges, who died about 1630, and whose monumental brass is at Wedmore, Somerset. The costume he wears (see accompanying illustration) is a buff coat girded with a sash, breeches of leather buttoned at the sides, and jack boots provided with spurs. The only remnant of defensive armour visible is the gorget of plate about the neck.

George Hodges, died about 1630. (From monumental brass at Wedmore, Somerset)

The introduction of knee-breeches as a garment generally worn by civilians occurred soon after the commencement of the seventeenth century. These garments were either buttoned at the sides or tied about the knees.

The effigy of a civilian, of about the year 1630, at Croydon, here given, is clothed in knee-breeches, a doublet with a skirt so short that it may more properly be called a lappet, plain falling collar and wristbands (instead of frills at the neck and wrists, as formerly), short cloak, with thrown-back collar or very small cape, and shoes.

The effigy of Elizabeth Culpeper (Ardingly, Sussex), 1633, may be taken as a good specimen of a lady's costume in the time of Charles I. The hair, it will be noted, is worn in flowing curls. A kerchief is thrown over the head, and falls down behind the figure. The

Civilian, *circa* 1630　　　Effigy of Elizabeth Culpeper,
(Croydon, Surrey)　　　1633 (Ardingly, Sussex)

use of striped material in sleeves and the richly ornamented front of the under-gown are worthy of note.

The Isham Collection, now in the Victoria and Albert Museum, contains a very good example of an

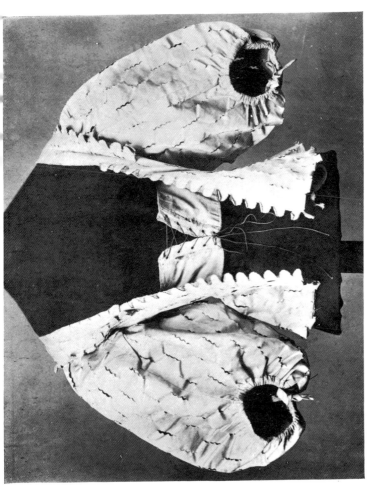

LADY'S BODICE OF CREAM-COLOURED SATIN WITH WAVY SLASHES

(EARLY SEVENTEENTH CENTURY)

SILK BROCADE GOWN OF THE TIME OF QUEEN ELIZABETH

early seventeenth century lady's bodice (here reproduced). The sleeves are full, and reach only to the
elbows, where they are drawn in by a cord. The front
is open, revealing a species of short stays laced by
a cord. The material is cream-coloured satin. It is
slashed with wavy cuts throughout at frequent intervals, and its edges are scalloped.

An interesting gown of woven silk brocade of the
Elizabethan period, from the famous Isham Collection,
is in the Victoria and Albert Museum. The ground of
the material is cream-coloured, and upon it coloured
groups of conventionally-treated floral designs have
been woven into it. The gown has a high collar, no
sleeves, no waist, and is slashed at frequent intervals
throughout its entire length. It falls gracefully in
well-developed folds from the yoke, which is plaited.
The general effect of this garment is extremely elegant.
It belongs probably to the end of Elizabeth's reign.
The back of the gown is shown in the accompanying
illustration.

The costume of the East Anglian yeoman in the
seventeenth century is well shown by monuments.
One, engraved in Cotman's book,[1] at Middleton
church, Suffolk, commemorates Anthony Pettow, yeoman, who died in 1610. He is represented in ruff,
fairly close-fitting, and plaited knee-breeches, tightly-
fitting tunic buttoned up the front, stockings, buckled
shoes, and a loose, open cloak with turned-down collar,
and with two buttons at each wrist. The tunic is

---

[1] *Sepulchral Brasses in Norfolk and Suffolk,* 1839, Vol. II, Plate
XXXIX.

drawn tightly to the waist by means of a belt fastening with a hook-clasp.   Altogether it is a simple but effective costume.

Some interesting information as to what kind of garments were worn by a fashionable and well-to-do young gentleman of the middle of the seventeenth century may be gleaned from the *Daily Expense-book of James Master*, from 1646 to 1676, which has been published by the Kent Archæological Society.[1]

The following are transcripts from 1646 to 1655 of such entries as relate to costume, together with the time of purchase and the amounts paid for the various articles.

This series of extracts will give a good idea of the general character of a gentleman's clothing of the period.

The extracts are limited to the first ten years of the Expense-book, because it seems undesirable to devote a larger proportion of the book to this particular subject, although there can be no doubt as to the great value of the information as illustrating the costumes of the period.

A few entries of special importance also are selected from the Expense-book subsequent to the year 1655.

1646		£	s.	d.
20 Nov.	For 2 pair of cordovan double seamed gloves . . .		6	6
11 Dec.	For 6 pa of band strings . .		2	0

[1] *Archæologia Cantiana*, XV, 152–216 ; XVI, 241–59 ; XVII, 321–52 ; XVIII, 114–56.

1646-47		£	s.	d.
2 Jan.	For 4 yards & an halfe of Spanish cloth for a sute & cloake at 23ˢ the yard .	5	3	0
,,	For an ell, quarter & halfe of Taffatye .		16	0
,,	For 2 bands & 2 pa of cuffs . .		5	0
,,	For 3 ya of black ribbon . .			6
4 ,,	For 28 yar of ribbon for points & tagging them	1	4	0
,,	For 8 yar. of silver ribbon at 15ᵈ ya .		10	0
,,	For 4 pa. of plaine boothose tops .		12	0
,,	For 3 ya. ¼ of silver lace weighing 2 own ¾		13	6
,,	For an hat		14	6
,,	For a white hatband . . .		3	6
8 ,,	For 2 pa. of ancle wosted socks . .		3	2
11 ,,	For a pa(ir) of perfumed gloves . .		2	6
13 ,,	For 4 pa of plane bands and cuffs .		10	0
14 ,,	For a pound of sweet pouder for linnen .		4	0
15 ,,	Paid to the Tailour for making my sad coulour cloath suit and cloake .	2	1	0
18 ,,	For a pa. of boots with goloshooes .		16	0
19 ,,	For halfe an elle of sarcenet . .		4	0
20 ,,	For a pare of silvered spurs . .		3	0
29 ,,	For vamping a pair of boots and given to ye shoomaker's boy . .		4	6
30 ,,	For soleing a pa. of boots . .		1	10
3 Feb.	For 2 pa of cordovan double seamed gloves		7	0
16 ,,	For a pair of black topps with gold and silver fringe		3	6
16 ,,	For 6 pa of linnen socks . .		3	0
17 ,,	For mending my black sute . .		5	0
,,	For a pa of halfe silk stockings . .		9	6
20 ,,	For ¼ of a yard of wrought satlin .		2	6
23 ,,	For a pa of perfumed gloves . .		2	6
,,	For 4 ounces of powder for haire .		1	0

H

1646–47		£	s.	d.
25 Feb.	Paid to my Tailour for making my lead coulor cloath sute with points .	2	15	0
20 Mar.	For new lining my college gowne .		13	3
3 April.	For a pair of thinne waxt shooes .		4	0
8 ,,	For 21 ya of 2ᵈ ribbon to trim my sute .		4	0
12 May.	For 3 yards of black ribbon . .		1	6
21 ,,	For vamping and colouring a pa of boots		5	0
12 June.	For a pa of Spanish leather shooes .		4	6
29 ,,	For mending my sute and my gowne .		3	0
19 July.	For a pa. of perfumed gloves . .		2	6
,,	For 3 ya of black ribbon . .			6
,,	For 8 ya of serge at 4/6 ya for a sute & cloake	1	16	0
,,	For an ell quarter & halfe of taffa at 12ˢ ell to line		16	6
,,	For 4 dozen and half of little silver lace weighing 10 ounces and a little over at 4ˢ 8ᵈ ye ounce	2	7	0
1647				
22 July.	For 3 pa. of plaine boothose . .		10	6
,,	For 2 pa. of threed stirrop hose . .		7	0
,,	For 2 pa. of gloves . . .		4	6
,,	For 8 ya of coloured gloves . .		4	0
,,	For black ribbon		2	0
19 Augᵗ.	For a pa. of red serge topps . .		6	0
,,	For a pa. of gray wosted stockings .		6	6
,,	For a pa. of black Spanish leather shooes		4	0
,,	For a pa of thinne waxt boots . .		12	6
16 Septᵗ.	For 2 ounces of powder for haire .		1	0
22 ,,	For a pa. of tan'd gloves & powder for haire		2	0
,,	For a shag hat & band . . .		6	0
1 Octʳ.	For a frock for my footboy . .		4	0
4 ,,	For 3 pa of threed ancle socks . .		4	6

1647		£	s.	d.
11 Oct^r.	For 6 bands and 6 pa of cuffs for my boy		7	0
,,	For new dying my hat . . .		1	0
13 ,,	For dying, dressing, facing & making up my cloake		14	0
11 Nov.	For a pa of waxt shooes . .		3	6
13 ,,	For a freeze coat for my boy . .		10	0
15 ,,	For 4 ya of gray cloath to make me a cloake	2	16	0
,,	For 2 ya of browne cloath to make me a sute	1	10	0
2 Dec^r.	For 3 pa of shooes for my footboy .		9	0
22 ,,	For making my serge sute wth 2 silver laces	2	12	0
,,	For makeing and byeing my frieze coate	1	3	0
,,	For byeing and making my footboys sute and cloake . . .	5	0	0
31 ,,	For 4 holland caps for my boy . .		1	6
1647–48				
6 Jan.	For soleing my waxt boots . .		1	8
10 ,,	For a pa of cordovan double seamed gloves		3	6
,,	For a ya & half of black ribbon . .			9
,,	For 2 half ells of lace for 2 caps .		5	6
18 ,,	For soleing my footboves shoes etc .		1	6
22 ,,	For vamping and soleing 2 pa of boots for my selfe		5	0
,,	For vamping a pa of boots for my footboy		2	6
10 Feb.	For a pa of grey woollen stockings for my footboy		3	6
15 ,,	For mending 2 pa of shooes for my footboy		1	6
16 ,,	For 17 ells ½ of frize holland at 4^s 6^d ye ell to make me 6 whole shirts & 4 caps	3	19	0

1647–48		£	s.	d.
2 Mar.	For an hat wth a black silke hatband .		17	0

1647–48		£	s.	d.
2 Mar.	For an hat wᵗʰ a black silke hatband .		17	0
21 ,,	For a pa of darke coloured boots .		12	0
,,	For making a sad colour cloath sute, & a gray riding cloake in November last	3	15	0
1 April.	For a cloake bag . . .		3	0
12 ,,	For vamping a pa(ir) of Spanish leather boots last summer . . .		5	0
21 ,,	For 6 ya of black ribbon . .		6	0
22 ,,	For mending & altering my footboys cloaths		7	6
27 ,,	For 11 ells of lockerum at 1ˢ 4ᵈ per ell to make my footboy 4 shirts & for thred		15	0
1648				
3 May.	For a pa of cordovan gloves . .		2	0
9 ,,	For a students gowne at secund hand .	1	8	0
13 ,,	For 6 holland plain bands & 6 pa of cuffs		17	0
,,	For a pa of band strings . .		8	0
15 ,,	For 2 pa of plaine boothose tops .		6	0
,,	For a black belt with a fringe upon it .		10	0
16 ,,	For a pa of scarlet wosted stockings for Jack		3	4
25 ,,	For 2 pa of shooes for my footboy .		6	0
27 ,,	For a band & a pa of cuffs . .		3	0
30 ,,	For a pa of gloves . . .		2	1
8 June.	For 8 ya & halfe of serge de roan for sute and cloak at 6s per yard . .	2	11	0
,,	For an elle & ¼ of Taffata to line my doublet		15	0
9 ,,	For a pa of white Spanish leather boots.		15	0
14 ,,	For 18 ya of 4ᵈ hair colour ribbon .		6	0
,,	For a pa of hair colour silk tops .		9	6
,,	For 2 pa of gloves . . .		2	6
15 ,,	For a pa of summer riding boots .		14	0

1648		£	s.	d.
15 June.	For a pa of Spanish leather shooes .		4	0
,,	For a pa of white riding tops . .		5	0
,,	For making a sad coulour serge sute & and cloath with buttons and buttonholes	3	6	0
16 ,,	For making 4 shirts for Jack &c .		2	0
26 ,,	For soleing Jack's shooes . .		1	2
29 ,,	For dressing an hat for my footboy .		1	0
10 July.	For a pa. of woollen stockings for Jack .		3	0
20 ,,	For 2 yar 3 quarters of gray cloath for a close coate at 14ˢ ye yard . . .	1	18	6
21 ,,	Given to ye tailour for making of it up .		15	6
9 Aug.	For 4 yards & an halfe of black cloath to make me a mourning cloake at 16ˢ ya	3	12	0
,,	For a black hatband, & a ya & a ha of black ribbon 2ˢ 6ᵈ. For wine 1ˢ 10ᵈ .		4	4
,,	For a pa. of trimmed mourning gloves .		4	0
17 ,,	For making my mourning sute & cloake	4	0	0
,,	For black ribbon to my old black sute .		2	6
18 Sepʳ.	For soleing my footboyes shooes .		1	0
4 Oct.	For vamping 2 pa of boots o . .		8	0
,,	For an ould pa. of boots for Jack bought of Mr Huggin		3	0
13 ,,	For dressing an hat . . .			
18 ,,	For an elle of Holland for 6 handkerchiefs		7	0
,,	For buttons to them . . .		1	0
20 ,,	For mending my footboys shooes .		1	6
27 ,,	For a pa of waxt shooes for myself .		4	0
,,	For a pa of waxt shooes for my footboy		3	6
2 Dec.	For making 2 pa of breeches & a doublet for Jack	1	9	0
1648–49				
3 Jan.	For vamping & coulouring a pa of black boots		4	0

1648–49		£	s.	d.
5 Jan.	For a pa of greene silk stockings .		19	0
27 ,,	For a pair of gray woollen riding stock-ings		6	0
,,	For a pa of black riding tops . .		4	0
,,	Given to Jack for wooll to mend 2 pa of stockings		2	0
6 Feb.	For dressing 2 hats . . .		2	0
19 ,,	For 2 pa of white gloves, & 1 pa of browne		5	0
26 ,,	For 6 pa of linnen socks . .		3	0
2 Mar.	For vamping a pa of boots . .		4	0
,,	For a pa of shooes for my footboy .		3	6
20 ,,	For soleing my footboye's shooes .		1	6
6 April.	For 6 holland pla. bands & 6 pa of cuffs		1	1
,,	For 4 pa of pla(in) boothose tops 2 gr at 11ˢ & 2 little at 6ˢ . . .		17	0
,,	For 4 pair of bandstrings . .		3	6
24 ,,	For 12 ells of fine holland, at 6ˢ ye elle to make me 4 whole shirts . .	3	12	0
,,	For 3 ya & an halfe of white bone lace .		10	6
7 May.	For setting up a pa of boots . .		2	6
24 ,,	For a pa of cordovan gloves . .		3	0
28 ,,	For 4 ya & ½ of Spanish cloath of a sad colour to make me a sute & cloake at 20ˢ p. ya. bought of brother Walsing-ham	4	10	0
30 ,,	For a pa. of halfe waxt boots . .		14	0
27 June.	For a pa. of Spanish leather shooes .		4	0
30 July.	For black ribbon . . .		5	0
4 Augᵗ.	For 4 ya & half of right french scarlet at 45ˢ	10	2	6
,,	For 3 ya. 3 quar. of serge de shaloon at 6ˢ ye yard	1	2	6
,,	For 2 ya. 3 quar of scarlet mohayr at 6ˢ		16	6

1648–49		£	s.	d.
4 Aug^t.	For 2 dosen & halfe of rich gold & silver flat buttons for my scarlet cloake at 19^s dos.	2	7	6
,,	For a dosen of tape buttons & a neck loop		4	6
,,	For 2 pa. of stirrop thred stockings .		6	6
10 ,,	For a silke hatband . . .		2	0
15 Sept.	For making my red cloake & stuffe sute &c.	4	15	0
26 ,,	For 2 yar. of Spanish cloath for a close coat	1	10	0
,,	For 19 ya. of gold & silver gallon lace weigh 11 ounces at 4^s 7^d per oun. to lace it	2	11	6
13 Nov.	For a pa of gray worsted stockings .		6	6
,,	For a pair of cordovan gloves . .		3	0
17 ,,	For a pa(ir) of waxt shooes . .		4	0
23 ,,	For vamping a pair of boots . .		4	0
30 ,,	For mending my cloaths & horse cloath		3	0
7 Dec.	For shagge french hat with ribbons .		12	0
8 ,,	For making my lace't coat . .		7	6
,,	For byeing & making my frieze coat .	1	7	6
24 ,,	For a pair of walking boots . .		11	6
,,	For dressing an hat . . .		1	0
1649–50				
29 Jan.	For a pa of white gloves & 4 ya of ribbon		5	0
30 ,,	For 3 ya of watchet sattin to make me a waistcoat	1	13	0
,,	For 4 ya. of gold & silver lace weighing 2 oun. & quarter to lace it . .		11	0
,,	For 72 ya of 6^d penny ribon to make 8 do(zen) of points . . .	1	16	0
,,	For 24 ya. of fancy ribon . .	1	0	0

1649–50		£	s.	d.
30 Jan.	For a pa of amber gloves and trimming them		4	0
,,	For tagging my points . . .		2	0
1 Feb.	For 4 yards & halfe of de Berry to make a coat	3	3	0
14 ,,	For a pa. of white gloves . .		2	0
16 ,,	For making my sad colour cloth sute & cloake with points . . .	3	0	0
,,	For making my sattin waistcoat & my great coat	1	15	0
,,	For a pa. of scarlet serge tops . .		4	0
18 ,,	For a leather belt wth a great silver fringe	3	0	0
6 Mar.	For a pa. of cordovan gloves . .		3	0
2 May.	For 18 ells of holland to make me 6 shirts at 5^s 2^d ye ell . . .	4	13	0
,,	For 1 ell of holland at 11^s 6^d ye ell .		11	6
,,	For 2 ya of bone lace to lace a band & cuffs	1	8	0
,,	For 2 ya. of lace for boothose tops .		11	0
,,	For 1 ya of little lace to put be ye cuffs .		2	0
,,	For 6 ya. of ribbon, a seale, & a po of plumms		6	0
9 ,,	For green ribon &c. . . .		2	6
11 June.	For a pa of Spanish leather shooes .		4	0
30 July.	For an English demie castor, band and hat case	1	7	0
6 Aug^t.	For 6 pa. of band strings . .		8	0
,,	For 1 fine pa of band strings . .		4	0
,,	For a great pa of boothose tops plaine .		6	0
,,	For a plaine band and cuffs . .		3	0
13 ,,	For 2 pa of gloves . . .		4	0
16 ,,	For vamping and colouring a pa of boots		4	6
,,	For a pa of halfe waxt boots & a pair of Spanish leather shooes . .		19	0

1649–50		£	s.	d.
13 Sep[r].	For 3 yards of ribbon		1	0
1 Oct[r].	For 18 ya of sattin & sil. ribbon for my sute	1	0	0
,,	For a pa. of jesamin gloves		4	0
,,	For 2 pa. of white gloves 2[s] 6[d]		2	6
9 ,,	For a leather hat-case		4	0
6 Nov.	For 20 ells of holland for 2 pair of sheets at 3[s] 3[d] ye elle	3	5	0
,,	For 2 ells of fine holland for 6 handkerchiefs & caps		13	6
,,	For a pa of tann'd leather gloves		1	6
8 ,,	For making my sad colour cloth sute	2	3	0
13 ,,	For 6 sett of handkerchiefe buttons		4	6
19 ,,	Paid to ye talour for making Jack's livery		15	0
21 ,,	For 2 sett of handkerchiefe buttons		2	0
25 ,,	For a pair of mild (mill'd?) hose		7	0
,,	For a pa(ir) of scarlet wosted tops		4	0
18 Dec.	For a pa(ir) of white gloves		1	6
,,	For lace for 2 caps		11	0
1650–51				
22 Jan.	For dressing my hat		1	0
27 Feb.	For a ya 3 qu. of Spanish cloath to make me a sute at 2[s] 6[d] ya	2	5	0
3 Mar.	For 2 pair of women's white gloves		2	4
29 ,,	For 12 yards of gold and silver ribbon		10	0
8 Apl.	For a pa of brown gloves & 4 ounces of haire pouder			
15 ,,	For 3 yards 3 quarters of red cloath to make my man a coat at 12[s] ye yard	2	5	0
,,	For 3 ya 3 qu. of ash colour baze to face it		7	0
25 ,,	For a shooting glove, brace &c		1	6
6 May.	For 6 yards of black ribbon		3	0

1650–51		£	s.	d.
10 May.	For a pair of tanned leather gloves .		1	8
3 June.	For 8 yards & a quarter of stuffe for a cloake at 6ˢ	2	9	6
,,	For 1 ya & 3 quarters of cloath to make me a sute at £1 6ˢ ye yard . .	2	5	0
1 July.	For 3 pa of gloves . . .		4	10
,,	For pouder for haire . . .		2	0
19 ,,	For a French shag hat and band .		14	0
,,	For a pair of linnen riding tops . .		4	0
24 ,,	For a demie Castor (beaver hat) .	1	7	6
31 ,,	For new dying my hat & a new lining tait		2	6
16 Augᵗ.	For making my sad colour stuffe cloake		17	0
26 ,,	For 12 yards of 2ᵈ black ribbon . .		2	0
27 ,,	For 17 ells of holland to make me 6 shirts at 5ˢ &c	4	5	0
4 Sepʳ.	For 4 ounces of haire pouder . .		1	0
16 ,,	For a pair of gray wosted stockings .		5	0
23 ,,	For an ell. 1 quarter and half a quarter of taffaty to line my doublet . .		16	0
,,	For 3 ya ¼ of Spanish cloath to make me a cloake	4	4	0
29 ,,	For 18 doz of silver buttons & a neck button at 2ˢ 8ᵈ ye doz. . .	2	10	0
,,	For 72 yards of 6ᵈ ribbon for points .	1	16	0
,,	For 24 yards of fancy ribbon . .	1	4	0
,,	For a pair of jessamin gloves . .		4	0
7 Oct.	For a French beaver (hat) . .	3	10	0
,,	For 1 yard 3 quarters & halfe of Flanders lace to make me band and cuffs .	3	0	0
,,	For a little lace for ye cuffs . .		6	0
,,	For 2 yards of lace for ye boothose tops	1	3	0
,,	For ye band, cuffs and boothose tops .		8	0
,,	For a band, cuffs and boothose tops of cambrick 11ˢ Spent a London 1ˢ .		12	0

1650–51		£	s.	d.
30 Oct.	For changing an hatcase, & a new white band		3	6
1 Nov.	For a greene taffatye quilt at second hand	3	10	0
4 ,,	For a pair of scarlet worsted halfe stockings		5	0
7 ,,	For a pair of gray serge tops and 2 ounces of Jessamin powder . .		7	0
12 ,,	For seweing ye lace on my coat &c .		2	0
14 ,,	For soleing a pair of shooes & shewing my bay mare		2	6
19 ,,	For making my cloth sute & cloake wth buttons	3	12	0
2 Dec.	For 18 yards of 4^d ribbon . .		6	0
,,	For a pair of sky-colour silke tops .		9	0
23 ,,	For a pair of tanned gloves . .		2	0
1651–52				
5 Jan.	For 7 ya & ha. of stuffe to line my cloake	1	10	0
4 Feb.	For a pair of Jessamin gloves . .		4	0
,,	For a lawne band & cuffs . .		4	6
5 ,,	For an elle of fine holland to make bands and cuffs		12	0
18 ,,	For black ribbons . . .		3	6
,,	For a pair of Worsted scarlet stockings		6	0
25 ,,	Paid for making my little coat . .		6	6
31 Mar.	For a pa. of black buckram stockings .		8	0
21 April.	For a pa. of tanned leather gloves .		3	0
21 May.	For a pair of holland boothose . .		5	6
,,	For 2 pairs of gloves 4 ounces of pouder & a pair of tuizers . . .		5	6
29 July.	For 1 pound & half of thred to make 2 pair of stockings . . .		4	6
27 Aug^t.	For a yard 3 quarters of Spanish cloath to make me a sute . . .	2	5	0

1651–52		£	s.	d.
27 Aug^t.	For 18 yards of silver lace weighing 14 ounces ½ to lace it . . .	3	5	0
,,	For a French demi-castor & white band	1	16	0
9 Sep^r.	For a pair of green silk tops and four ounces of pouder . . .		10	6
24 ,,	For an oyled hat case & a box combe		3	6
18 Oct.	For knitting 2 pair of stirrop hose and 2 pair of socks . . .		7	6
26 ,,	For a pair of gray wosted stockings and a pair of white gloves . . .		7	6
18 Nov.	For a periwig		16	0
,,	For making my lace't sute . .		14	0
23 ,,	For a pounde of haire pouder . .		3	0
,,	For dressing my hat . . .		1	0
7 Dec^r.	For a pair of waxt shooes setting up and colouring a pair of boots . . .		7	6
14 ,,	For 3 pa of gloves, & 3 yar. of black 8^d ribbon		9	0
23 ,,	For a perriwig		15	0
,,	For a pa of white serge stockings laced .		15	0

1652–53				
20 Jan.	Paid to Jolly for pairs of boots and 3 pairs of shooes . . .	3	5	0
3 Feb.	For 9 dozen of ribbon to make 12 doz of points at 6^d ol. ye yard . .	3	1	0
,,	For 24 yards of fancy ribbon . .	1	4	0
,,	For a pair Jessamin gloves . .		3	6
,,	For a leaden plate for my hat . .		4	0
,,	For a perriwig & new curling of another		17	0
10 ,,	For a pa of sea-greene silke tops & a pair of band strings . . .		12	0
18 ,,	For 2 quilted caps		6	6
21 ,,	For mending my cloths . . .		1	6
2 Mar.	For 6 pair of women's white gloves .		9	0

1652-53		£	s.	d.
2 Mar.	For a pair of women's green silke stockings		16	0
14 April.	For 2 pair of linnen boothose . .		12	6
18 May.	For 9 yards & ½ of stuffe to make me a sute & coat	1	15	0
,,	For a new perriwig . . .		16	0
,,	For 3 ells & ½ of sarsnet to line ye dublet & coat	1	15	0
,,	For 3 dozen of satin ribon at 10ˢ ye dozen	1	10	0
,,	For a lawne band & cuffs . .		3	6
,,	For 4 pair of linnen socks . .		2	6
,,	For a pair of Spanish leather shooes .		4	6
8 June	For 17 ells of holland to make 6 shirts at 4ˢ 2ᵈ ye elle	3	10	10
14 ,,	For a pair of black taffata boothose .		13	0
2 July.	For a leather belt . . .		4	6
,,	For a pair of Spanish leather shooes .		4	6
8 ,,	For a pair of black silke tops & black gloves		11	6
,,	For 5 yards of black ribbon 8ᵈ ye yard .		3	6
23 ,,	For making my sad colour cloth sute & cloake wᵗʰ buttons . . .	6	3	0
,,	For a pair of black gloves . .		1	6
12 Augᵗ.	For a pa of gray worsted stockings & a pair of black gloves . . .		8	0
,,	For an oyled hat case . . .		2	0
10 Sepʳ.	For 2 pa of white gloves . .		3	0
12 ,,	For 2 pa of shooes . . .		8	0
17 ,,	For a new perriwig & curling 3 other .	1	0	0
19 Octʳ.	For a pair of shooes & vamping 2 pair of boots		12	0
11 Nov.	For soleing a pair of shooes . .		1	0
21 ,,	Paid to ye taylour for making my stuffe sute & coat & my 2 mourning sutes .	11	0	0
23 ,,	For 5 yards of stuffe to make me a coat	1	15	0

1652–53		£	s.	d.
23 Nov.	For 3 yards of serge to line it . .		11	6
,,	For 3 ya. of black ribbon . .		2	0
29 Dec.	For a pair of gloves & spent at London		4	6
1653–54				
13 Jan.	For 2 cambrick bands & 1 pair of cuffs .		6	0
24 ,,	For 3 pair of gloves & a pair of slippers		8	6
,,	For new dying 3 hats & spent at London		7	6
26 ,,	For a new periwig & curling 4 others .		19	0
,,	For a pair of white serge tops . .		3	3
,,	For a pair of Spanish leather shoos and goloshooes		8	0
8 Mar.	For a French demi castor & silk band .	2	6	6
15 ,,	For a pound of haire pouder . .		2	0
14 April.	For a pair of women's silke stockings .		16	0
,,	For a new laceing and dying my riding hat		5	6
29 ,,	For a pair of riding gloves and a whip .		6	0
3 May.	For 14 yards of serge to line my chariot at 3ˢ 10ᵈ ye yard . . .	2	13	6
,,	For 18 ounces & halfe of silke fringe at 2ˢ 4ᵈ ye ounce	2	3	0
9 June.	Paid to ye Talour for my close stuffe coate & my mourning sute wᵗʰ points	6	8	0
,,	For a pair of watchet silk tops & a pair of gloves		11	6
16 ,,	For a new border of haire & curling 2 others		14	0
20 ,,	For 2 pair of linnen boothose & a plain band and cuffs		17	0
,,	For a pa of gloves & spent at London .		10	0
27 ,,	For a pair of shooes . . .		4	6
,,	For 6 pair of linnen socks . .		3	6
1 July.	For 2 cambrick bands . . .		4	0
,,	For an elle of fine holland . .		11	0

1653-54		£	s.	d.
1 July.	For a pound of linnen pouder . .		5	6
26 Aug^t.	For a pair of shooes & 3 yards of black ribbon		6	6
,,	For a pair of gloves . . .		3	0
,,	For an ounce of Jessamin butter and 3 ounces of haire pouder . .		3	6
15 Sep^r.	For a pair of shooes & given to George Cock		5	6
11 Nov.	For a pair of shooes & goloshooes .		8	0
1 Dec.	For a pair of gray worsted stockings .		9	0
2 ,,	For a livery coat for my man . .	1	12	6
9 ,,	For 18 ells of freeze holland at 6ˢ 8ᵈ ye elle to make me 6 shirts . .	6	0	0
20 ,,	For 2 pair of gloves & 2 ounces of haire pouder		7	0
21 ,,	For 2 pa. of boothose tops 1 pair holland ye 2ᵈ lawne		10	0
29 ,,	For a pa. of white worsted stockings .		7	0
,,	For a pa of white gloves & 3 yards of black ribbon		3	6
1654-55				
26 Jan.	For a pair of spurrs & 4 ounces of haire pouder		4	0
19 Feb.	Paid for making my cloath sute with black ribbons	4	2	6
16 Mar.	For a French demi caster (beaver hat) .	2	5	0
31 ,,	For a pa. of Cordovan gloves . .		3	0
14 April.	For a belt with silver buckles . .	1	0	0
,,	For a pair of gloves & 3 yards of black ribbon		8	6
,,	For a pair of Jessamin gloves & a pair of fr cizers (scissors) . . .		6	0
,,	For a pa of Spanish leather shooes .		4	6

1655		£	s.	d.
12 May.	For an elle of fine holland to make bands		14	0
,,	For an elle & quarter of holland to make 6 handkercheifs . . .		9	0
,,	For 3 garnish of handkercheife buttons		3	0
17 ,,	For a pair of shoe strings . .		2	6
18 ,,	For 17 yards of gold drugget to make me a sute & coat & line ye dublet at 12^s ye yard	10	4	0
,,	Paid to Mr. Snead for making my gold drugget sute & coat & for an hat band	3	18	0
19 ,,	For a pair of Spanish leather shooes .		4	6
26 ,,	For half a pound of haire powder & an ounce of Jessamin butter . .		4	6
12 June.	For setting up a pair of boots . .		4	0
13 ,,	For 3 garnish of handkerchief buttons .		3	0
2 July.	For a pair of greene silke stirrop hose .		16	6
14 ,,	For a pair of sawne little boothose .		6	6
4 Aug^t.	For a pair of fring'd linnin riding boot-hose		8	0
,,	For a pair of kid's gloves & halfe of haire pouder		4	6
11 ,,	For a pair of waxt shooes . .		4	6
16 ,,	For a pair of waxt shooes . .		4	6
7 Sep^r.	For 12 yards of 2^d ribbon & a black cap		3	9
14 ,,	For a pair of Spanish leather shooes .		5	0
18 ,,	For 2 lawne bands . . .		3	6
24 Oct.	For halfe a pound of haire pouder .		2	0
3 Nov.	For 2 Cambrick bands 2 pair of cuffs 2 pair of boothose tops & leggs & 1 pair of french band strings . . .	1	10	6
9 ,,	For a french Demie Castor & band .	2	6	6
,,	For dying & lining another & for a leather hat case . . .		9	0
16 ,,	For 11 yards of black camelet. de Holland to make me a sute & cloake (at 10^s ye yard)	5	10	0

		£	s.	d.
1655				
16 Nov.	For 2 yards & half of white Tabye to line the doublet	1	2	6
,,	For 7 yards & ¾ of black velvet to line ye cloake at £1 5^s ye yard . .	9	11	6
24 ,,	For a pair of gray worsted stockings wth tops		8	0
,,	For a pair of white wollen stirrop hose .		2	6
,,	For a pair of blush colour silk stirrop hose woven		15	6
,,	For 36 yards of blew & silver sattin ribbon at 14^d ye yard . . .	2	2	0
,,	For a pair of Jessamin gloves & making my shooe strings . . .		5	6
19 Dec.	For 4 yards & ½ of Camelett de Holland to make me a coat . . .	1	9	0
,,	For 4 yards of serge to line it . .		14	0
20 ,,	For a pair of Jessamin gloves & a pair of white gloves		4	6
,,	For a pound of Jessamin pouder & a pair of white gloves . . .		6	6
21 ,,	For 4 yards of gray Spanish Cloath to make me a sute and coat at £1 6^s ye yard	5	4	0
,,	For 2 lawne bands & 2 pair of cuffs .		7	0
,,	For 4 yards of silver ribbon . .		4	0
24 ,,	For a black fringed belt . . .	2	15	0
,,	For a pair of white serge riding stockings		6	6
1656				
12 April.	For a yard and ¼ of Scotch cloath to make my footboy 6 handkerchiefs at 16^d ye yard		1	8
,,	For 10 ells of Lockeram to make him 4 shirts at 14^d the ell . . .		11	4
13 June.	For 2 pair of threed stirrop-hose, & a pair of anckle socks . . .		8	6

I

		£	s.	d.
1656				
21 Nov.	For 5 yards of Kentish Cloth to make my footboy a sute & coat, & my groome a coat . . .	3	0	0
1656-57				
17 Jan.	For spinning 2 pounds of wooll for Jack's stockings		1	4
,,	For knitting 2 pair of stockings for Jack		2	6
1657				
6 June.	For 8 yards of serge de Roan to make me a sute & coat at 3^s 6^d ye yard .	1	8	0
,,	For 6 yards & ½ of French Taby to line the sute and coat at 7^s 6^d the yard .	2	8	0
,,	For 42 yards of black and silver lace weighing 6 ounces & ½ and 3 drams at 4^s 4^d per ounce to lace sute and coat	1	9	0
8 ,,	For a pair of pearle colour silk stockings	1	2	0
,,	For a pair of black garters and shooe strings		10	0
13 Nov.	For 4 yards of Spanish cloth to make me a sute and coat . . .	5	0	0
,,	For 9 yards of Taby to line the sute & coat at 7^s 6^d per yard . . .	3	7	0
1663				
28 May.	Paid for a Perrewig . . .	5	0	0
30 ,,	For a new cap for my Perriwig . .		3	0

Some useful lists of the seventeenth century garments and materials, with the prices paid for them, have been printed by Rev. Dr. J. Charles Cox in *The Ancestor*, Nos. 2 and 3, under the title of *The Household Books of Sir Miles Stapleton, Bart.*, but there is no space for extracts in the present volume.

QUILTED AND RICHLY ORNAMENTED YELLOW SATIN GOWN OF
ABOUT THE YEAR 1725

CHAPTER IX

EIGHTEENTH CENTURY COSTUME

THE costume of the eighteenth century, if lacking in the refinement and grace of earlier times, was distinctly quaint and picturesque. During the reign of Queen Anne the fashion was in the direction of square-cut coats with ample skirts and long, ample waistcoats descending to the knees in such a way as to conceal the breeches, which were worn with long stockings. Pockets, cuffs, and buttons were strongly marked features of the coat. Garters, buckled shoes, a white cravat, shirt with gathered-up cuffs at the wrists, cocked hat, and long, flowing wigs completed the male attire during the first half of the century.

In the accompanying illustration is shown a dress of quilted and richly ornamented yellow satin, with quilted white satin under-gown or "fore-part" wrought in elaborate floral designs. The sleeves have turned-back cuffs, and are shaped to the arm. The upper part of the gown has a turned-back collar and is cut low. The gown is believed to belong to the earlier half of the eighteenth century, perhaps about the year 1725, and is an excellent example of the dress of the period.

THE COCKED HAT

The cocked hat, as we now know it from the dramatic
and pictorial representations of Dick Turpin and other
highwaymen of ancient times, is a type of a very large
class of hats.   It is lineally descended from the high-
crowned hats which were in favour during the reigns
of Elizabeth and James I, and which lingered on until
the time of Charles II.   Before the latter period, however, the rim became remarkably broad, and when
much worn or exposed to rough and windy weather,
it was liable to hang down in an uncomfortable fashion
close to the head.   At that stage the hats were commonly known as slouched hats.   The broad-brimmed
hat, surrounded with feathers, prevailed in the reign
of Charles II, and continued during a great part of
that of William III.   But, from the inconvenience of
the broad brim, one flap was made to be cocked up,
and was placed either in front or at the back of the
head.

The advantage of this arrangement was at once seen;
and another part of the rim was fastened up, making
a hat with two upturned flaps.   About the time of
Queen Anne, the third flap was introduced, which
formed the complete cocked hat.

It thus becomes apparent that this particular form
of head-gear had no special significance in itself, but
rather that it grew out of the undue proportions which
the hat-rims of the seventeenth century had assumed.
In the middle of the eighteenth century the cocked hat
was worn as a mark of gentility, professional rank,

and distinction from the lower orders, who wore them uncocked.

The cocked hat, cocked at two points, still continues to be the correct head-gear for Court dress and for high ranks in the Army and Navy.

An ancient specimen of the cocked hat was for many years worn by the President of the Society of Antiquaries upon the occasion of the formal admission of a new fellow, and, although the practice of actually wearing it has ceased, the hat is still placed on the table before the President at every meeting of the Society.

WIGS

In the strict sense of the term these were hardly, perhaps, parts of costume, but it will be convenient to deal with them in this place.

The history of the periwig begins during the time of Queen Elizabeth or a little before. What is believed to be the earliest mention of it in England is an entry among the Privy Purse expenses of Henry VIII, where the item "for a perwyke for Sexton the King's fool, 20 shillings," occurs under the date of December, 1529. In the middle of the sixteenth century they were very generally worn, and towards the end of the century the demand for hair for making them had become so great as to render it dangerous for children to wander about alone, as it was common for them to be enticed away and deprived of their hair.

In the middle of the seventeenth century periwigs of immense size were worn by the clergy as well as the laity.   It is a curious fact that the wearing of such large periwigs had an important and lasting effect on certain articles of ecclesiastical attire, the episcopal chimere and the parson's surplice both being opened in front in order to accommodate them.

In order to keep these enormous periwigs in good order, small, slightly hollowed cylinders of pipe-clay were made hot and used as a kind of shape for winding the long curls upon.   These objects, of which large numbers are found in London and other large centres of population, are called wig-curlers, bilboquets, and roulettes.   They were often called "pipes" from the fact that they were made of pipe-clay, and the use of these warmed roulettes with a wig, in order to restore the crispness and neatness of its curls, was in the eighteenth century called "to put a wig in pipes."

The *Daily Expense-book* of James Master, from which a series of extracts is given above, affords several interesting glimpses of the growing fashion of wearing the wig.

Thus, under the date 18 November, 1652, we find an entry of the payment of sixteen shillings for a periwig.   On the 23rd of the following month the sum of fifteen shillings is paid for a periwig.   In the following February a periwig and new curling of another cost seventeen shillings.   On the 18th of May following, a new periwig is purchased for sixteen shillings. In September of the same year one pound is expended on a new periwig "and curling 3 other."

As time went on, it is clear that the wigs became more elaborate and more expensive, for a "perrewig"

PART OF THE EFFIGY OF SIR WILLIAM SCAWEN, 1722, IN CARSHALTON
CHURCH, SURREY

purchased in May, 1663, cost Mr. Master no less than £5.

Our modern word wig is a corrupt and abbreviated form of the French perruque, and has passed through many changes of form, including perwyke, perriwigg, periwinkle, etc. Dr. Johnson, who of course wore a periwig, gives the following amusing definition of it : "Perewig (péruque *Fr.*)—Adscititious hair, hair not natural, worn by way of ornament or concealment of baldness."

The various forms of wigs of the eighteenth century were known by a great variety of names,[1] including—

> The pigeon's wing.
> ,, comet.
> ,, cauliflower.
> ,, royal bird.
> ,, staircase.
> ,, ladder.
> ,, brush.
> ,, wild boar's back.
> ,, temple.
> ,, rhinoceros.
> ,, corded wolf's paw.
> Count Saxe's mode.
> The she-dragon.
> ,, rose.
> ,, crutch.
> ,, negligent.
> ,, chancellor.
> ,, cut bob.
> ,, long bob.
> ,, half-natural.

[1] See *The London Magazine*, 1753.

The chain buckle.

  ,, corded buckle.

  ,, detached buckle.

  ,, Jasenist bob.

  ,, drop-wig.

  ,, snail-back.

  ,, spinach seed.

  ,, artichoke.

     etc., etc.

"Bob-wigs," "bag-wigs," "campaign wigs," "tra-velling wigs," etc., were other forms.   The cauliflower wig was a rather shapely, close-cropped wig, much affected by the clergy.   Dr. Jeremiah Milles, Dean of Exeter, who died in 1784, is represented as wearing such a wig in the excellent portrait bust belonging to the Society of Antiquaries, at Burlington House.[1]

The extravagances of the fashionable world in the second half of the eighteenth century are well shown by some beautiful gowns for ladies' wear preserved in the Museum at Stockholm.   In one splendid example of a court dress, comprising a richly ornamented kirtle, a closely fitting bodice ending in a stomacher-like point, and an outer gown, open in front, extending only just so far as to be visible on each side near the hips, the sides of the dress are distended to a total width of nearly five feet.   This dress was made in 1751. In another lady's court dress of the year 1766, the hip improvements are even more angular and pronounced,

---

[1] The wig lingered on as part of the episcopal costume beyond the middle of the nineteenth century.   Dr. George Murray, Bishop of Rochester, who died in 1860, is believed to be one of the last of the English episcopacy to wear the wig.

STAY BUSK, INSCRIBED E.E. 1776

the projections on either side extending in a perfectly horizontal line at the level of the waist for a total distance of nearly six feet. The bodice descends in an even more pronounced point than in the earlier dress, and the outer skirt leaving, as before, almost the whole of the under-skirt, or kirtle, open in front. The total width of this distended gown on a level with the hips is considerably greater than the height of the whole garment, from the hem to the top of the bodice.

This development of dress in the direction of narrowing the waist and extravagantly widening the hips is a curious recurrence of the fashion prevalent during the reign of Queen Elizabeth, and well shown in some of the portraits of that sovereign, particularly in that showing her at the age of fifty-nine, in the possession of Viscount Dillon, at Ditchley.

One of the most remarkable leaders of fashionable, fast life in the West of London during the eighteenth century was Madam Teresa Cornelys. She was the daughter of an actor, and the wife of a public dancer. Although a woman of scandalous life, she managed in 1760 to purchase Carlisle House, in Soho Square, and here she gave a series of subscription masked balls which, in the course of time, grew so famous as to attract wide attention and support. On one occasion it is recorded that the Duke of Gloucester and half the peerage were present. From the period when she took Carlisle House (1760) to the date of her failure (1772) her assemblies and concerts were attended by men and women dressed in all the absurdities of the macaroni and other extravagant fashions.

Many of the costumes worn on these occasions were remarkable only for their peculiarity—thus, one man appeared as half miller, half chimney-sweep ; another as Adam, dressed in flesh-coloured silk and an apron of fig-leaves. But many of the ladies wore dresses of the most costly character, and some were decked in jewels to the value of from thirty to fifty thousand pounds.

Towards the end of the eighteenth century it was the fashion for both ladies and gentlemen to wear two watches, the short chains of which hung down from the waist-belts in the case of the ladies, and from small pockets or fobs in the breeches of the gentlemen.

The gentlemen of the day wore their wigs clubbed, that is, made into a kind of club-shaped mass, and muffs of large size were worn even at the theatre.

The importance of the muff as an article of fashionable costume in the year 1787 is indicated by the fact that one of blue fox varied in price from a guinea and a half to ten guineas, and muffs of natural black fox were offered for sale and bought at prices ranging from four guineas to fifty guineas.

MACARONI COSTUME

The period between 1770 and 1775, roughly speaking, was marked by one of the most extraordinary and monstrous eccentricities of head-dress, in both ladies and gentlemen, which the world of fashion has ever witnessed. During the prevalence of that fashion, it was no uncommon thing for ladies to keep their head dressed for a month at a time without disturbing the

A MACARONI

absurd arrangement of gauze wire, ribbons, and flowers with which the hair was kept into the desired form and decorated. The various contrivances to which the votaries of this craze had recourse, in order to obtain rest for the head without disarranging the structure which was built upon it, would be laughable were it not a humiliating reflection that any one should make themselves look so foolish in order to comply with the requirements of *la mode*.

"The Macaronis," for so these extravagantly dressed individuals were called, had a club in London, to which were admitted certain curly-haired and spy-glass-bearing young men who, having done some travelling, had picked up and adopted some of the eccentricities of foreign customs. Goldsmith justly sneers at them—

> Ye travell'd tribe, ye macaroni train
> Of French friseurs and nosegays justly vain.

And Boswell, in his *Tour to the Hebrides*, speaks of them in equally satirical language: "You are a delicate Londoner; you are a Macaroni; you can't ride."

A contemporary magazine points out that the term was introduced into England in connection with the well-known Italian article of food. It was imported at Almack's as an improvement on the ordinary subscription-table, "and, as the meeting was composed of the younger and gayer part of our nobility and gentry who, at the same time that they gave in to the luxuries of eating, went equally into the extravagances of dress, the word Macaroni then changed its meaning to that of a person who exceeded the ordinary bounds of fashion ; and is now justly used as a term of reproach to all ranks of people who fall into this absurdity." This was written in 1772, but the popular estimation of a Macaroni must have fallen still lower at a later date, for in one definition, written nearly half a century afterwards, we find him described as "a coarse, rude, low person."

The Macaroni was the fop or dandy of his day, but unfortunately the absurdities of his costume were not confined to his own sex. The ladies adopted the Macaroni style, and their chief aim seemed to be to vie with each other in the magnitude and extravagance of their head-dress.

It is not to be wondered at that the caricaturists and wits of the day made fun of these absurdities. Indeed, the Macaronis made fun of them themselves, introducing them in their most widely extravagant forms into masquerades.

They paraded the walks of Hyde Park, exciting the ridicule of every beholder. Upon the top of his head the Macaroni wore an exceedingly small cocked hat, with gold button and loop, and a gold tassel on each side, to preserve its equilibrium. Coat, waistcoat, and breeches were all equally short and tightfitting ; the last being frequently of striped silk, with large bunches of ribbon at the knees. The cane, often used to lift the hat from the head, was as fantastic as the rest of the costume : it was generally of portentous length, and decorated with an abundance of silk tassels. Large bunches of seals and chains attached to two watches, a white necktie fastened under

the chin with an immense bow, white silk stockings
in all weathers, and small shoes with diamond buckles,
completed the attire.

Some of the extravagances of the eighteenth
century costume are detailed in the following lines,
written in 1776 :—

> Give Cloe a bushel of horsehair and wool,
>   Of paste and pomatum a pound,
> Ten yards of gay ribbon to deck her sweet skull,
>   And gauze to encompass it round.
>
> Of all the gay colours the rainbow displays,
>   Be those ribbons which hang on her head,
> Be her flounces adapted to make the folks gaze,
>   And about the whole work be they spread.
>
> Let her flaps fly behind, for a yard at the least,
>   Let her curls meet just under her chin ;
> Let those curls be supported, to keep up the jest,
>   With an hundred, instead of one, pin.

It is a noteworthy fact that the end of the eighteenth
century, which witnessed the grotesque outburst of
extravagance in the shape of the Macaroni fashion,
a phase which may be regarded as the final development of the older fashion, witnessed also the introduction of a new style, scarcely less absurd, in the form
of the tall hat.

THE TALL HAT

The tall hat, one of the most remarkable and uncomfortable parts of modern attire, was first publicly worn
in London on 15 January, 1797. The first to introduce

the fashion of wearing it was John Hetherington, a
haberdasher residing in the Strand, London. The
result of wearing such a startling novelty in head-gear
was that a large crowd of spectators gathered round
the haberdasher before he had proceeded far along the
street. Hetherington was arraigned before the Lord
Mayor on a charge of breach of the peace and in-
citing to riot, and was required to give bonds in the
sum of £500. The evidence produced went to show
that Mr. Hetherington, who was well connected, appeared on the public highway wearing upon his head
what he called a silk hat (which was produced), a tall
structure having a shiny lustre, and calculated to
frighten timid people. As a matter of fact, the officers
of the Crown stated that several women fainted at the
unusual sight, while children screamed, dogs yelped,
and a young son of Cordiwiner Thomas, who was
returning from a chandler's shop, was thrown down by
the crowd which had collected, and had his right arm
broken.

One of the London newspapers, in commenting on
this curious commotion over the introduction of a new
hat, regards the innovation as "an advance in dress
reform, and one which is bound, sooner or later, to
stamp its character upon the entire community. The
new hat is destined to work a revolution in head-gear,
and we think the officers of the Crown erred in placing
the defendant under arrest."

It seems open to question whether the tall hat was an
entirely new invention of the eighteenth century, because it is quite possible that the idea may be traced to

the high, conically crowned hats worn in the reigns of Queen Elizabeth and James I, and described as sugar-loafed hats, or high copt hats. These early high-crowned hats were in fashion until the reign of Charles II, but meanwhile their form had undergone much modification. Immediately after the reign of James I there was a tendency to make the brim much broader and the crown lower. The "cocked hat," in which these inconveniently broad brims were fastened up to the side of the crown, was the natural sequence in the development. (See COCKED HAT).

A kind of compromise between the cocked hats of the eighteenth century and the tall hats of the nineteenth century may be still seen in the high stringed hats now worn by bishops and doctors of divinity.

THE MUFF

The muff has long been, as it still remains, an important article of feminine attire. Like so many other parts of a lady's costume, there can be no doubt that it was originally intended for the useful purpose of protection from the inclemencies of the weather and the retention of the natural heat of the body. It was, of course, particularly intended to shield the hands, wrists, and, to a limited extent, the body from cold and wintry winds, but it soon became an article of clothing quite as much for adornment as for utility.

During the latter part of the eighteenth century muffs were worn by gentlemen as well as ladies, and this not merely in the streets in winter or when skating on the ice, but even at the playhouse. Moreover, they were made of enormous size, and they must have appeared as inartistic as they were useless accessories of dress in a warm theatre.

Muffetees were small muffs or mittens worn around the wrists. They were made of either fur or worsted, and of various colours.

A satirical song on male fashions in the time of Queen Anne mentions scarlet and green muffetees as worn by men at that time.

An early eighteenth century beau is thus summed up by D'Urfey in *Wit and Mirth* (1706) :—

> A wig that's full,
> An empty scull,
> A box of burgamot ;
> A hat ne'er made
> To fit the head,
> No more than that to plot ;
> A hand that's white, .
> A ring that's right,
> A sword-knot, patch and feather ;
> A gracious smile,
> And grounds and oyl,
> Do very well together.

The allusion to the hat not fitting the head clearly refers to the fashion of the period for beaux to carry the hat under the arm, not on the head, so that the large powdered periwig might not suffer thereby.

Hoop petticoats were very fashionable in the early part of the eighteenth century, and one of the earliest ballads referring to the custom was one written about the year 1733, commencing :—

What a fine thing have I seen to-day ;
    O mother, a hoop !
I must have one, you cannot say nay ;
    O mother, a hoop !
For husbands are gotten this way to be sure,
Men's eyes and men's hearts they so neatly allure,
    O mother, a hoop, a hoop ! O mother, a hoop !

The following description of a fashionable lady's costume in the year 1754 is extracted from *The Universal Magazine* of that year:—

The dress in the year fifty-three that was worn
Is laid in the grave, and new fashions are born ;
Then hear what our good correspondents advance,
'Tis the pink of the mode, and 'tis dated from France ;
Let your cap be a butterfly, slightly hung on,
Like the shell of a lapwing just hatch'd, on her crown ;
Behind, like a coach horse, short dock'd cut your hair,
Stick a flower before, screw, whiff, with an air ;
A Vandyke in frize your neck must surround,
Turn your lawns into gauze, let your Brussels be blond,
Let your stomacher reach from shoulder to shoulder,
And your breast will appear much fairer and bolder ;
Wear a gown or a sacques, as fancies prevail,
But with flounces and furbelows ruffle your tail ;
Set your hoop, show your stockings and legs to your knees,
And leave men as little as may be to guess :
For other small ornaments do as before,
Wear ribbands a hundred, and ruffles a score ;
Let your talk, like your dress, be fantastick and odd,
And you'll shine at the Mall ; 'tis taste a-la-mode.

K

CHAPTER X

MEDIÆVAL AND LATER GARMENTS

THERE are many mediæval garments whose names and forms are forgotten by the fashionable world of the present time. In the case of some we still possess survivals either in form, or name, or both: but the majority have undergone so much modification as to be utterly unlike the originals which we see in contemporary representations of mediæval costume. In the present chapter brief descriptions will be found of some of the more interesting, important, and little-known garments of the Middle Ages and more recent times.

BARBE

This was a piece of linen, pleated into folds, worn by widows over or under the chin, and falling straight down to the breast. It was worn as part of the dress of ladies in mourning as well as by actual widows, and was in vogue during the fourteenth and fifteenth centuries. From the "Ordinance for the Reformation of Apparell for the good Estates of Women in the tyme of Mourning" (Harleian MS., 6064), made by Margaret, Countess of Richmond, mother of Henry VII, we learn that the barbe was permitted to be worn above the chin in the case of the Queen and all ladies down to the rank of a baroness. The daughters of lords and knights were required to wear the barbe below the chin ; whilst persons of lower rank were to wear it on the lower part of the throat.

By the end of the seventeenth century, and probably somewhat before that period, the barbe had come to be a mask or vizard.

BOOTS AND SHOES

The various forms of coverings and defences for the feet at different periods present a great many changes and modifications of patterns. From the earliest times, probably, the feet were enclosed in some kind of protective covering formed of the skins of animals. The Romans, as we know from several examples which have been preserved, as well as from statuary and other sources of information, made their shoes of leather cut into many open-work devices. Mr. Charles Roach Smith has figured examples in his *Catalogue of Roman Antiquities found in London*, and there are numerous specimens in the Guildhall Museum, and in private collections. The Anglo-Saxons appear to have constructed their shoes on Romano-British models, but they also had high boots called socca, extending halfway up the calf of the leg, formed of leather, and falling in wrinkled creases. Some of those figured in illuminated manuscripts appear to have been laced up the front from a point beginning almost close to the toes. The Norman shoes as shown in the Bayeux Tapestry were made to cover the feet only. They had a kind of rolled-over top encircling the leg just above the ankle, lace-holes and laces extending to the toes, and either no heels or very small heels. The soles of this early type of shoes were often made of wood.

After the Norman Conquest shoes were of various colours, probably coloured leather, including yellow, blue, green, and red, and they became richer as time advanced.

Chausses, a term especially used for armour for the legs, was also used to indicate the pantaloons or tight coverings for the legs and feet, introduced from France.

Many extravagant and fantastic forms of boots or shoes were worn during the reign of William II, and as time advanced their points were made more and more extravagantly long. During the reigns of Henry I and Stephen peak-toed boots and shoes, provocative of satire and ridicule, became the vogue for lay folk, although they were not permitted to be worn by the clergy.

A curious type, fashionable at this period, was that known as pigacia, the points of which resembled the tail of a scorpion. Another variety was that known as the cornado, in which the curl of a ram's horn was simulated.

In the fourteenth century the shoes worn exhibited exaggerated right and left tendencies, the point immediately beyond the great toe being lengthened, whilst the curve on the outer side of the foot was strongly marked so as to show the precise outline at that point.

The extravagant length of the toes of shoes reached its greatest development, perhaps, during the reign of Richard II, a period which was remarkable for elaborate and costly costume. At this epoch the long toes of boots and shoes are said to have been attached to the knees of the wearers in order to make walking a possible exercise.

In a monumental effigy at Margate, Kent (that to Nicholas Canteys, who died in 1431), some good examples of shoes are represented, in which the whole of the surface of the leather is powdered with stars of various sizes, and the fastening is by means of lacing up the sides.

Another example, also of the reign of Henry VI, is to be found in a brass of a franklin in Faversham parish church, Kent. In this instance the boots are fastened in front by means of two straps and buckles. Boots reaching somewhat higher up the leg, and fastened in front by four sets of straps and buckles, are

Boots, *circa* 1480

represented in an interesting monument in Elford Church, Staffordshire, of about the year 1480.

In the next example here figured we have a spurred, defensive boot of the year 1568 from the monumental brass to Sir Richard Molyneux at Sef-

Boot and spur, 1568

ton, Lancashire. The slipper-

like shoe from the monumental brass to William
Hodges, 1590, at the church of Weston-sub-Edge,
Gloucestershire, is an interesting form of the latter
end of the century in which the crude markings may
represent cuts or slashings in the leather.

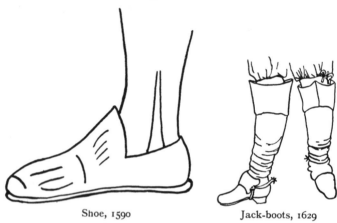

Shoe, 1590   Jack-boots, 1629

The brass to Sir Edward Filmer, at East Sutton,
Kent, depicts some good examples of jack-boots of the
year 1629, a type which underwent many variations
during the seventeenth century.

A valuable illustrated account of boots and shoes
at various periods of history may be found in the
Viscount Dillon's edition of Fairholt's *Costume in
England*, Vol. II.

CASSOCK

The original form of the cassock seems to have been
that of a long, loose gown, but the term has been used
loosely and vaguely. By some it has been regarded
as a loose kind of military cloak worn by soldiers,

thrown open to display the armour in fair weather, and buttoned up to protect it when the weather was likely to injure the armour, or when for any reason it was desired to conceal the armour.

The cassock was worn by women as early as the fourteenth century. In the reign of Henry VII "mourning cassocks" are mentioned as being worn by ladies and gentlemen.

As an ecclesiastical garment the cassock is well known, and will be dealt with at a later stage.

CHILDREN'S COSTUMES

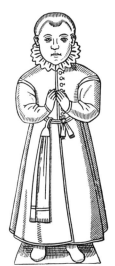

There are two admirable illustrations of the costumes of children depicted in monumental brasses at Merstham Church, Surrey. The effigy of Peter Best, 1585, shows the pretty little dress of a child, with a ruff at the neck, and a handkerchief suspended from the girdle. The other child, Richard Best, 1587, is dressed in "swath-bondes," or swaddling clothes, with a hood pinned over the head, and a plaited bib pinned over the breast.

Peter Best, child, 1585 (Merstham, Surrey). He has a handkerchief tied at his girdle

Richard Best, 1587 (Merstham, Surrey)

COAT

The coat seems to have been first known in England by that name in the fifteenth century. By a gradual process of change the coat may be said to have been evolved from the vest or long outer garment worn towards the end of the reign of Charles II. The lower part of the sleeves of this garment were adorned by a turned-back cuff, and sometimes the sleeves were fulled and puffed. During the reign of James II the coat became a very popular garment. As the length increased the sides were found to be inconvenient, and the corners were accordingly fastened back (sometimes with a button) to keep them out of the way. This was very apparent in the military costumes of the last century. It does not appear that the sides of the coat were cut away until the reign of George III.

The two buttons at the back of a modern coat are an interesting survival of those buttons which in former times assisted to support the sword-belt. They speak of a time when swords were worn as much by private individuals as by members of the military and naval professions.

The various changes and modifications through which the coat has passed, from the vest of the time of Charles II to the familiar form of our own day, would afford a sufficient theme for a long chapter, but as space does not admit of that, it will only be possible to touch briefly upon the subject.

The points of the coat-collar turned back on the breast remind one of the eighteenth century method,

GENTLEMAN'S COAT AND TRUNKS, EARLY EIGHTEENTH CENTURY

(FROM THE ISHAM COLLECTION)

by which the bottom corners were turned up and fastened out of the way by buttons. The same thing has clearly happened to the upper corners, which were turned and buttoned back out of the way of the chin. The surviving fashion of facing these turned back corners with silk is another trait which recalls the old fashion, and, in fact, represents the material with which the garment was originally lined.

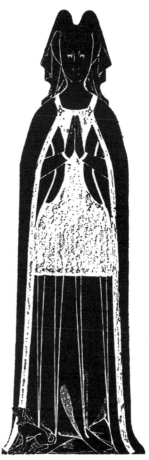

COTE-HARDIE

This garment was a tight-fitting tunic buttoned down the front, and reaching nearly half-way down the thigh, worn by both sexes during the fourteenth and fifteenth centuries. Ornamentation in the form of a row of buttons is found round the lower end of the cote-hardie, whilst an elegantly ornamented girdle was usually worn over it, encircling, not the waist, which might be considered the most natural position, but the hips. In the case of gentlemen this girdle or belt supports a small dagger or anelace.

Lady, 1458 (Jamina de Cherneys, Lady-in-waiting to Queen Margaret of Anjou and wife of Sir Thomas Sherborne)

Ladies wore the cote-hardie of greater length, sometimes reaching to the feet.

The sideless cote-hardie, which was a very fashionable female garment in the Middle Ages, is represented in various stages of development, in the series of effigies figured by T. and G. Hollis and Stothard. Many of the monumental brasses published by the brothers Waller and in the portfolios of the Monumental Brass Society, and various handbooks on the subject, are equally useful. It will obviously be impossible and unnecessary to refer to more than a very small proportion.

The earliest of the monumental brasses to show this garment is the memorial to Sir John de Creke and lady, at Westley Waterless Church, Cambridgeshire, the date of which has been supposed by good authorities to be about the year 1325. The lady wears a kerchief and wimple. Her undermost garment is a closely fitting gown ; over this is a cote-hardie with the sides cut away all round the arm. These edges, as well as the edges of the mantle throughout, are decorated by an inner line which gives an invected or scalloped appearance. Fortunately, the mantle is widely opened in front, so that it is possible to see the arrangement of the dresses quite well. The material of the cote is quite thin, and from a fold which is brought under the right hand one can see that the cut in the side of the garment extends from over the shoulder almost to the waist.

The effigy of Lady Montacute (in Oxford Cathedral), so famous for other details of costume, also shows a remarkably good example of a sideless cote-hardie. The date of the monument (1354) indicates the development of the fashion at about the middle of the fourteenth century. The cuts on each side are edged with an extremely rich ornament of formal foliated work. The material of which the cote is constructed is of the most beautiful description. The ground colour is a rich rose-pink, and over it is a pattern of powdered leopards' heads, roses, and perhaps vine leaves and scrolls, the latter in green, the former in yellow and pink. Anything more beautiful in the form of a mediæval garment is almost inconceivable.

Ornamentation round the opening on each side of the cote-hardie was evidently a great feature in the latter part of the fourteenth century, and the method of wearing the mantle open suggests that the ornaments were intended to be seen and admired. A good example is to be found on the brass to the wife of Sir Thomas Walsh, died 1393, at Wanlip church, Leicestershire.

FARTHINGALE

This curious article of attire is practically contemporary in its origin with the ruff; in other words, it came into use a little before or at the accession of Queen Elizabeth, and continued in vogue, with some extraordinary developments, during her long reign, reaching its most exaggerated form in the time of Anne of Denmark, the second queen of James I.

At first the farthingale was bell-shaped, being small at the hips and broadening out considerably as it descended. By the end of the sixteenth century it became much developed on the hips, and assumed what has been called the "wheel"-shape.

The farthingale, which may be regarded as the prototype of the eighteenth century hoop, and the crinoline and "dress-improver" of more modern times, was clearly in its origin a contrivance for displaying to the best advantage the rich and costly fabrics used for the dresses of the period. In process of time, however, it is equally clear that the farthingale was admired by people of fashion for its own shape, and for the proportions it imparted to the various parts of dress. This is indicated by the fact that the fully developed farthingale was invariably accompanied by a long, stiff, and pointed stomacher (see STOMACHER), the effect of which was to emphasize the breadth and bulk of the farthingale.

FRONTLET

The frontlet was a strip or band of cloth, silk, or velvet, often richly ornamented, worn by ladies over the top of the head and descending on each side of the face down to the waist. (See HEAD DRESSES OF LADIES.)

GLOVES

The early history of gloves is involved in some obscurity. Planché, in his *Cyclopædia of Costume*, remarks that gloves do not appear to have been worn in England before the end of the tenth or the beginning of the eleventh century, and probably they were of German manufacture. These early gloves were

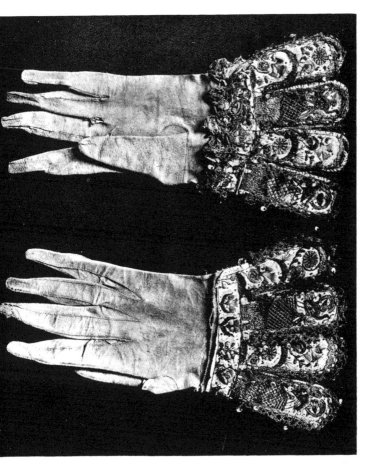

PAIR OF GLOVES OF THE REIGN OF QUEEN ELIZABETH

MADE OF LIGHT BROWN LEATHER, AND THE GAUNTLETS ARE OF WHITE SILK EMBROIDERED
WITH SILVER THREAD AND STRIPS AND SPANGLES

very rare and costly, and were worn only by the most exalted personages. There is confirmation of this in the fact that gloves form part of the coronation garments of the English sovereigns and are also part of episcopal vestments.

Before gloves came into common use the hands were kept warm by means of the long sleeves of the gowns.

Fairholt, in his *Costume in England*, points out that even "in the fourteenth century gloves were commonly worn with long tops, and carried in the hand or thrust beneath the girdle," so that at that early date they had ceased to be entirely articles of utility and convenience, and had become parts of fashionable costume.

Gloves were sometimes worn in the hat in the Middle Ages, and with three distinct meanings, viz. as the favour of a mistress, the memorial of a friend, and the challenge to an enemy.

Episcopal gloves were woven throughout and adorned with embroidery and jewels. The accompanying sketch is from the monumental brass to Robert Wyvill, Bishop of Salisbury. The gloves represent the type worn by bishops in the year 1375.

The actual gloves of William of Wykeham, Bishop of Winchester, who died in 1404, still exist at New College, Oxford, where they are treasured as relics of one of the most powerful and remarkable men of his time, a man who was not only a great builder, and a distinguished dignitary of the Church, but also Lord Chancellor of England. Wykeham's gloves, which are woven of faded red silk, have on the back the

sacred monogram "I H S" in a circle surrounded
by the rays of the sun.

The gloves of Queen Elizabeth are preserved in the
Bodleian Library at Oxford.   One glove of Mary
Queen of Scots is preserved in Saffron Walden
Museum.   Others which once belonged to the same
Queen are in the Ashmolean Museum, Oxford.   One
of the gloves of James I, made of crimson silk, is in
private possession.   In all these royal gloves the
fingers and the chief part which covers the hands have
been left unornamented, but fringe and elaborate embroidery enrich the gauntlets, or those parts which
surround and reach a considerable distance up the
wrists.

The gloves commonly worn by ladies and gentlemen of the period extending from the reign of Elizabeth until the end of the eighteenth century, generally
appear to have ornamented gauntlets, and probably
they did not differ greatly from those of royal personages of the time, except in richness of material and
elaboration of ornament.

An excellent example of gloves of the period of
Queen Elizabeth, from the Isham Collection, is in the
Victoria and Albert Museum (see the accompanying
illustration).   The gloves are of light brown leather,
with deep gauntlets of white silk embroidered with
coloured silks, silver gilt and silver thread, and also
strips and spangles.   They are edged with silver-gilt
lace.

There are a good many interesting survivals of the
former symbolical meaning associated with the wear-

ing of gloves. White, and sometimes laced, gloves have, by a very ancient custom, been presented at a maiden assize. A blow given with a glove was long considered a gross affront and tantamount to a challenge to fight a duel. The wearing of gloves by the clergy when preaching is another curious survival, and although now very rare, if not actually extinct, was certainly in existence in country districts, in the recollection of the present writer, within the last thirty-five years.

Much valuable information upon the subject of the history of gloves will be found in a book entitled *Gloves: Their Annals and Associations*, by S. W. Beck, 1883.

HEAD-DRESSES OF LADIES

Women's head-dress, for many centuries past, has occupied a foremost place in the fashions of wealthy and well-dressed people. The varieties of form, size, and materials which from time to time came into vogue were numerous, and they are excellently depicted on monumental brasses and sepulchral effigies.

There is in the churches of England a long series of brasses representing the effigies of women, in which the development of the head-dress from the early part of the fourteenth century down to the seventeenth century may be traced. Old fashions die out, and new fashions take their place, with a regularity of succession all over the kingdom which affords a most instructive and interesting insight into the various waves of fashion which originated in France or elsewhere and soon influenced the fashionable circles of England.

Before glancing at this series of effigies engraved on brass, however, it may be convenient to begin with the earlier figures in illuminated MSS.

The evidence for the costume of ladies prior to the earlier years of the fourteenth century consists of illuminated MSS., sepulchral effigies, and other carvings. In the magnificent illuminated Psalter executed for Robert of Lindsey, abbot of Peterborough from 1215 to 1222, and now preserved, as one of the finest existing English manuscripts of its time, in the library of the Society of Antiquaries of London, we find a very charming head-dress worn by the Blessed Virgin Mary. It consists of a loosely setting wimple covering little of the neck and sides of the face, a kerchief covering the top of the head and kept in position by a closely fitting stiff band round the head. This band has at two visible places pointed additions suggestive of the ornaments of a coronet. The wimple and kerchief are both, apparently, of thin, fine material. The head-dress is very simple and decidedly graceful, and, from the history of the manuscript, must be of quite early thirteenth century date.

Another source of information on this subject is the fine series of sculptures adorning the west front of Wells Cathedral,[1] the period of which extends from about 1220 to 1240. In the lower tier of figures there is a statue, believed to represent St. Mary Magdalen with her box of ointment, whose head is covered with a tightly fitting stiff band, whilst a kerchief forms a species of loose wimple hanging from the band on the

[1] See *Archæologia*, Vol. LIX, pp. 143, 206.

head. There are two or three other female head-dresses
resembling this, and in more than one case there is a
distinctly-represented band passing tightly under the
chin, and so arranged, apparently, as to securely fix
the head-dress upon the head.

A still clearer illustration of the details of this species
of head-and-chin-band head-dress is to be found in the
effigy of a lady, apparently of the latter end of the
thirteenth century, in Romsey Church, Hampshire.

The earliest of the head-dresses of women shown on
brasses is that commemorating Margarete de Camoys,
about the year 1310, at Trotton Church, Sussex. This
is a graceful and well-proportioned piece of work.
The figure wears an ample cote-hardie, a kirtle with
tight-fitting, buttoned sleeves, a wimple covering the
point of the chin and the ears, and a veil and kerchief
(or coverchief) enveloping the whole of the upper part
of the head and falling down to the shoulders in
delicate folds which indicate a fine and probably quite
soft material. The hair, which is confined across the
forehead by an ornamental fillet, is allowed to appear
on either side of the brow in the form of small single
curls. The outer garment, or cote-hardie, had once
been ornamented by nine shields of arms, all of which
have been stolen.

Another very similar effigy is that of Lady Joan de
Cobham, of about the year 1320, in Cobham Church,
Kent. Further specimens exhibiting practically the
same style of head-dress are (i) on the reverse of a
palimpsest brass at Norbury Church, Derbyshire, representing, probably, Matilda, wife of Sir Theobald de

Lady of Sir John de
Creke, about 1325
(Westley Waterless,
Cambridgeshire)

Verdun, died 1312, and buried in
Croxden Abbey; (ii) a half-effigy of
a lady, of about the year 1350, at
Upchurch, Kent; and (iii) the effigy
of the wife of Sir John de Creke,
1325, here figured.

Another development relating to
the arrangement of the head-dress
was the plaiting of the hair on either
side of the face somewhat in the form
of ears of corn. This form of hair-
dressing is found in connection with
the sleeveless cote-hardie.

The next stage in head-dress is that
known by the terms zigzag, nebulé,
or reticulated forms. This kind really
consists of close caps or cauls in
which the hair is enclosed. The terms
zigzag and nebulé indicate a species
of waved frills ; the reticulated form,
as the word indicates, was a kind of
network sometimes jewelled. An excellent example of the wavy, or nebulé,
kind of caul is represented in the
brass to Maud Lady de Cobham,
who died about the year 1360. The
brass forms one of the superb series
in Cobham Church, Kent. The caul
encloses the hair of the whole of the
head down to a point lower than the
ears. Here a short length of hair is

visible, and it falls upon the shoulders, where it is again gathered up into a kind of net or caul of zigzag form. This lower caul appears as two small protuberances over the shoulders. There is another lady's effigy at Chrishall, Essex (Joan, wife of Sir John de la Pole), of about the year 1370, with almost identical head-dress; and there are several others. A small toy dog is generally represented at the feet.

The effigy of Dame Margaret de Cobham, died 1375, has another very interesting coiffure in which the nebulé caul encloses all the hair on the head reaching down almost to the shoulders, and allowing only a very small portion of the hair to remain visible. No terminal caul is to be seen in this example.

The distinction between the nebulé and the regular zigzag caul is believed to be a mere technical variation in draughtsmanship, or engraving, and hardly requires to be considered from the point of view of costume.

As the end of the fourteenth century is approached, the caul is made smaller, reaching, in the case of Dame Margaret de Cobham (Cobham Church, Kent), died 1395, only to the top of the ears. That this is not a local peculiarity is shown by the fact that other similar examples exist at Broughton, Lincolnshire; Ore, Sussex; Dyrham, Gloucestershire; and St. Mary's Church, Warwick.

There are many examples of reticulated head-dress shown on monumental brasses. The following may be mentioned :—

Lady Margaret D'Eresby, Spilsby, Lincolnshire, 1391.

Dame Katherine Walsh, Wanlip, Leicestershire, 1393.

Dame Dionisia Attelese, Sheldwich, Kent, 1394.

Dame Alicia Cassy, Deerhurst, Gloucestershire, 1400.

Dame Elianor Mauleverere, Allerton Mauleverer, West Riding, Yorkshire, 1400.

A lady, Elizabeth ——, Goring, Oxfordshire, 1401.

During the latter years of the fourteenth century the crespine style of head-dress was introduced.   This consisted of a network of gold or silver-covered threads jewelled at the intersections, in which all the hair was enclosed at the top of the head.   Over this head-dress was worn a small kerchief in such a way as to fall down behind the head, and also to slightly overlap in front. A jewelled fillet was usually worn across the forehead with this head-dress.

The following effigies afford excellent examples of the crespine head-dress :—

Elyenore Corp, Stoke Fleming, Devon, 1391.

Margaret, wife of Thomas Lord Berkeley, Wotton-under-Edge, Gloucestershire, 1392.

Dame Lora St. Quintin, Brandsburton, Yorkshire, 1397.

Ele Bowet, Wrentham, Suffolk, 1400.

Dame Margaret Pennebrygg, Shottesbrooke, Berkshire, 1401.

There are numerous early fifteenth century examples of effigies wearing the crespine head-dress in which the hair is bunched up at the sides of the head above the ears ; and by about the year 1415 the caul of this particular kind of coiffure was made larger, and of squarer shape, in such a way that the ears became covered. In the course of a few years the caul assumed a very grotesque form, the terminations being curved outwards and upwards in such a way as to resemble a pair of horns. This was the origin of the various kinds of head-dresses which are now known by the names horned, mitre, lunate, and heart-shaped.

Many specimens of this species of dressing the hair exist in English church monuments, and the fashion was evidently deservedly popular for some years. It is considered probable that the fashion was set by the head-dress being worn by Isabella of Bavaria, queen of Charles VI of France. When worn in moderate size it is far from inelegant, but occasionally it was carried to great and absurd extremes, as was the case in the

Effigy of Millicent Meryng, about 1415 (East Markham, Notts)

brass effigy to Jane Keriell, about the year 1460, Ash, near Sandwich, Kent, in which the caul is carried upwards in the form of a large horse-shoe, and no veil is worn. Veils are also wanting in the case of some groups of daughters placed below their parents.

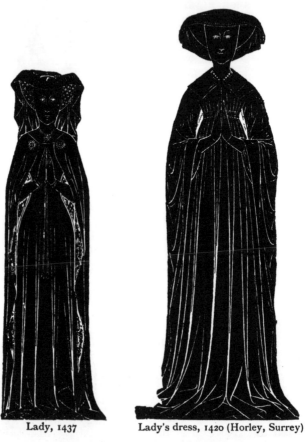

Lady, 1437   Lady's dress, 1420 (Horley, Surrey)

In the brasses to Lady Tiptoft and Powis (about 1470) at Enfield, Middlesex, and Isabel Plantagenet, daughter of Richard Earl of Cambridge (1483), at

PORTRAIT OF MARGARET, QUEEN OF JAMES 3RD OF SCOTLAND
(MARRIED IN 1469 : DIED 1486)

Little Easton, Essex, the horned head-dress is surmounted by a coronet.

The next form of head-dress, the butterfly as it is
significantly called, assumed even more remarkable
proportions than the horned variety, and whatever
it may have looked like when actually worn on the
head as a fashionable piece of dress,
one must feel bound to admit that on
effigies it appears out of all just proportion to the rest of the attire. It was
introduced in or about the year 1470.

It is not an easy task to give an
exact account of the origin, development, and disappearance of each of
these types of head-dress. That they
are more or less closely related and, in
spite of their variations, bridged by
some kind of transition is made sufficiently clear by the evidence of the
effigies themselves.

The styles shown on the effigies on
monumental brasses already described
cover a space which extends from the
early years of the fourteenth century

Effigy of Anna Play-
ters, 1479 (Sotterley,
Suffolk)

to about the end of the fifteenth century, and during
that period there is much overlapping of the different
styles. This, indeed, is inevitable when new fashions
are introduced from time to time and taken up by the
wealthy, and all the while old fashions continue to be
worn by those to whom change is distasteful as well
as by those whose means are small.

The head-dress known as the hennin was worn by ladies of France and Flanders in the fifteenth century. Generally, it may be described as of a high conical shape, with a muslin veil hanging down from it. It was sometimes nearly two feet in length, and the point extended backwards from the head, so that the thin gauze veil hung in graceful folds behind the shoulders.

The fine portrait of Margaret of York, third wife of Charles the Bold of Burgundy, painted by Memlinc, shows in an excellent manner the method of construction of a head-dress in the latter half of the fifteenth century. The head-gear belongs to what is usually called the heart-shaped style, and rises to a considerable height above the forehead. Behind there is an ample veil of very fine material, which falls and spreads out to the width of the shoulders. A portion of this fine gauze is brought entirely over the head-dress proper, passing straight from one ear to the other in a line which intersects the eyebrows at four points.

The excellent portrait of the same person in the collection of the Society of Antiquaries of London, which is elsewhere described in this volume, may be compared with Memlinc with advantage. The head-covering in the picture, the date of which is probably 1468, is more of the regular pointed steeple-like type, but made of black material.

The head-dresses hitherto considered were supplemented by still another style during the last decade of the fifteenth century. This was the well-marked type or rather group of head-coverings known by the various

EFFIGIES OF SIR WILLIAM SMYTHE, KNIGHT (CIRCA 1525) AND HIS TWO
WIVES, ANNE STAUNTON AND ISABELLA NEVILLE, ELFORD CHURCH,
STAFFORDSHIRE

but descriptive names pedimental, pyramidal, kennel, and diamond-shaped head-dress. The chief feature of these forms is the gable-like form of the strip of material which borders the face. This strip itself is made much larger than formerly. It is bent at a sharp angle over the centre of the head and again on each side about the region of the ears, whence it falls straight down nearly to the waist. A good example of the pedimental head-dress and frontlet of a lady of the year 1533 is here shown. This strip or band is called the "frontlet." It was usually highly ornamented with embroidery work, and sometimes studded with jewels. The long frontlets reaching to the waist, or nearly so, have the effect of giving a rather formal, melancholy expression to the counten-

Lady's head-dress, 1533

ance of the wearer, and it may have been for this reason that the next fashion, much in vogue during the reign of Henry VIII, was in the direction of shortening the lappets and giving them an outward curve. There are numerous portraits which illustrate this in an admirable way. Among them are those of several of the queens of Henry VIII and other portraits painted by Holbein.

A brass at Bletchingley, Surrey, dated 1541, shows this head-dress well.

In the portraits of Lady Jane Grey, Queen Mary, and Queen Elizabeth a new and very charming feature in head-dresses makes its appearance, namely, the French hood, a type which, as the name suggests, is due to foreign influence. It would be difficult to find a more graceful and pleasing form of head-gear than

Lady's head-dress, 1541

this French hood, which is perhaps more particularly associated in the public mind with the portraits of a not altogether popular person, Queen Mary. It is also found in the earlier and simpler costumes of Queen Elizabeth before she succeeded to the throne. Several of the portraits of Mary Queen of Scots[1] show charm-

---

[1] See *Notes on the Authentic Portraits of Mary Queen of Scots*, by Sir George Scharf and Lionel Cust, 1903.

ing examples of it, both with and without a border of frilling between the hood and the head. Portraits of Mary Queen of Scots when a widow, with a white wimple and head-dress of the French-hood type, exist in the royal collection at Windsor Castle, and in the Bibliothèque Nationale at Paris ; and there is an excellent profile portrait of the Queen in later life in a medallion by Primavera, in which the exact method of wearing a flowing veil behind the head, hanging down from the French hood, is admirably shown.

A lady of about the year 1580 (Staplehurst, Kent)

Amongst less exalted folk the French hood was very commonly worn for a considerable part, mainly the second half, of the sixteenth century. Representations of it in monumental brasses are general, and it is fortunate that the heads of ladies there shown are generally depicted with a slight turn to the right or left, by which means the veil, or in some cases the lappet, hanging behind is visible. (See the accompanying head-dress from a brass at Sefton, Lancs, dated 1568). An extraordinary specimen is seen in the brass to Elizabeth Crispe at Wrotham, Kent, the date of which is 1615.

Here the hood is made of immense size, spreading out
into very large curves on each side, the veil brought
round the shoulders and hanging down below the
waist at the back like a cloak.　Another less remarkable example is at Ardingly, Sussex, in the brass to
Elizabeth Culpeper, 1633.

By the beginning of the seventeenth century it had
become the fashion to bring the lappet from the back

Lady's head-dress, 1568

of the hood forward over the top of the head, producing a curious flatness which can hardly be considered graceful or pleasing.　The examples in the
brasses to Aphra Hawkins, at Fordwich, Kent, 1605,
and Mary Leventhorp, at Sawbridgeworth, Hertford-
shire, 1600, show this feature very well.

In the early part of the seventeenth century the
steeple-like, high-crowned, brimmed hat makes its
appearance as an addition to the regular head-dress
of ladies.　The material appears to have been of a soft

pliable nature, as is shown by the irregularity of the
outline of the brim, which, by the way, is sometimes
pointed in front. There is usually a wreath round the
crown. (See the accompanying sketch from a brass at
Writtle, Essex, dated 1616.) The general belief is that
hats of this type were worn by country folk and

Lady's head-dress and ruff, 1616

adherents to the Puritan party, rather than in the more
fashionable circles. Although simple, these hats are
distinctly graceful in form, and they add considerably
to the picturesqueness of the ladies' costume at the
time, which usually included ruffs for the neck and
huge farthingales.

HERALDIC MANTLES

The arms of a knight were often displayed on the garments he wore.   The principal of these was the

tabard, a kind of sleeveless coat worn over the armour.   These are found represented on brasses about the beginning of the fifteenth century, and are always represented as covered with armorial devices.

Armorial or heraldic mantles were also worn by ladies.   An excellent example of such a mantle in a brass of the year 1518 is here shown.

HUKE, HUYKE, HEWK, OR HUYCK

This was a species of cape or cloak furnished with a hood.   There appears to have been more than one meaning, as there was more than one form, to the term.   The

Effigy of Elizabeth Knevet, 1518 (Eastington, Gloucestershire).   She wears a heraldic mantle

huke at one time signified a cloak or mantle worn by women and afterwards by men; but subsequently it was applied to a tight-fitting dress worn by both sexes.

HOUPPELANDE

This is a name which was sometimes given to a fur-lined tunic with open hanging sleeves, resembling those of the surplice, and drawn in at the waist by means of a girdle, which was sometimes ornamented. It was worn by both men and women in the earlier half of the fifteenth century. It probably came first from Spain, and was then brought over from France. Good representations of it are found in various monumental brasses in English churches. In some cases the houppelande was enriched with fringe round the lower hem and an elaborate girdle and collar. The sleeves are shown hanging open and lined with fur.

The chief characteristics of this garment were its ample, comfortable proportions and the looseness with which it fitted the body of the wearer. It was made of two lengths, one reaching only to the middle of the thigh, the other descending to the ankles. In some cases the collar was small, rising as a slight ridge round the neck, but it also was made broad enough to fall over in a fold.

An example of the houppelande with large surplice-like sleeves brought in close at the wrists, lined with fur and descending to the ankles, occurs in the brass to John Lethenard, 1467, at Chipping Campden, Gloucestershire.

There is some uncertainty as to the origin and precise meaning of the word houppelande, Planché favouring the idea that it was derived from the Spanish hopalanda, meaning "the train of a gown worn by students," but the *New English Dictionary*, under the simple form houpland, declares it to be a word of unknown origin.

HOSE. SEE LEG-COVERINGS

JACK

This was a protective garment, resembling the brigandine in being formed of metal plates enclosed between two sheets of canvas. The jack was particularly the garment of the ordinary soldier, because it was much less costly than plate armour.

Originally the term "jack" was applied to a loosely fitting coat or tunic of jacked leather, hence its name. It is sometimes known as a "leathern jack." (See JACKET.)

JACKET

The jacket, although (as we now understand the term) merely a sort of small coat, is in reality quite a distinct garment, not merely in name, but in origin and ancestry also. The word is a diminutive form of "jack," a loose coat or tunic, made originally of jacked leather, whence its name. This was, of course, a military garment, and when stuffed and quilted, was the usual coat of defence of the archers and crossbowmen of the fifteenth century. It was made rather full, reaching as far as the knees, whereas most other military garments for the body were made to fit closely. At what time the smaller jacket came into general use as a part of a civilian's costume it is impossible to say ; but there is reason to think that it was at a somewhat remote date.

Jackets have for many years been worn by the middle and lower classes, and their convenient form and protective qualities against the cold have caused them to be very generally adopted by labourers in the place of the old-fashioned but picturesque smock-frock or round-frock which is now only worn by shepherds and cowmen in out-of-the-way districts.

KERCHIEF

The kerchief was essentially a head-covering, a cloth composed of linen or richer material (sometimes silk or even fine gold-cloth), for covering the heads of women. It was in vogue among the Anglo-Saxons, who called it heafods-rægel, or head-rail. It is also called coverchief, kercher, and kerchief. It is interesting to note how this name, which really belongs to nothing but a head-covering, has been in later years applied to the familiar accessories of costume known as the handkerchief, the pocket-handkerchief, and also the neck-handkerchief, the last-named use indicating practically a revival of the original idea of a covering. The use of the word handkerchief is believed to date from the sixteenth century.

KIRTLE

The term "kirtle" is one which has been applied to a great variety of garments worn by both sexes at different periods during the Middle Ages and later. Strictly, however, it may be defined as a loose gown. Originally the kirtle, it is believed, was a short linen under-garment, a fact which is borne out by the name given to the article, kirtle being sometimes written curtel, which is equivalent to short.

Chaucer, whose descriptions of English costume afford invaluable illumination on many obscure points in the names given to different parts of dress, speaks thus of the kirtle :—

"in my kirtle bare";
"Syngle in a kertyl";
"Their kerteles were of inde sendel";

from which we may infer that in his day, the latter half of the fourteenth century, the garment was of fine material and intended for under-wear.

The *New English Dictionary* offers one or two interesting definitions which must be accepted with reserve in view of the conflicting and even contradictory character of the available evidence. They comprise: (1) A man's tunic or coat, originally a garment reaching to the knees or lower, sometimes forming the only body-garment, but more usually worn with a shirt beneath and a cloak or mantle above. (2) A woman's gown. A skirt or outer petticoat. (3) A coat or covering of any kind.

LEG-COVERINGS

The various forms of garments used as leg-coverings by men at different periods have been known by many different names, such as trews, trousers, hose, breeches, stockings, etc., and the whole system of nomenclature has been very much confused. There has been a natural development of form, and the new names introduced to indicate the different changes of fashion may not always, perhaps, have had a precise meaning. To take one term only with its qualifications, we find that hose, according to the *New English Dictionary*, means "an article of clothing for the leg ; sometimes reaching down only to the ankle as a legging or gaiter, sometimes also covering the foot like a long stocking." But, as a matter of fact, the term is generally used nowadays to indicate stockings. Half-hose is a term which means short stockings, or socks. The latter term by a natural process of association has come to be applied to an additional, movable foot for the boot or shoe.

In the times of Elizabeth and James I the fashionable leg-coverings in use consisted of (1) trunk-hose, a term synonymous with breeches, particularly the padded variety, and (2) nether-hose, which was equivalent to the modern word stocking. The two parts were united by a number of decorated ties called points. This arrangement for the fastening together of various parts of dress is referred to on more than one occasion in Shakespeare's plays. Thus in *Henry IV*, First Part (Act II, scene 4), Falstaff says :—

"Their points being broken—"

and Poins interrupts, in order to make a joke, with—

"Down fell their hose."

Long hosen were also fastened to the jacket or doublet by means of a species of points or latchets called herlots. In this way the whole of the legs were entirely encased in hosen, sometimes made of the finest velvet.

Boot-hose is a term which appears to have more than one meaning. "Boot-stocking" is the brief explanation given in the *New English Dictionary*, but Dr.

Johnson's definition is at once clearer and fuller—he says: Boot-hose.   Stockings to serve for boots: spatter-dashes," and in the illustrative quotation he gives from Shakespeare (*Taming of the Shrew*, Act III, scene 2) the meaning is more fully explained :—

> " His lacquey, with a linen stock on one leg, and a boot-hose on the other, gartered with red and blue list."

Hose may be regarded as the usual term indicating the leg-coverings in use during a good part of the Middle Ages, and superseded at the beginning of the sixteenth century by trunk-hose or breeches.   Stocks and stockings, in consequence of the new garments then introduced, were called hosen, but as a distinctive garment the stocking has an antiquity extending back to the Anglo-Saxon period, when they were made to reach from the knee downwards.   In illuminated MSS. of that period stockings are usually represented as falling in irregular oblique wrinkles from the knee to the boot, where they are lost to view.   The Anglo-Saxons also had a stouter species of leg-covering, made of leather, to which the term skin-hose was applied.

LIRIPIPE

This was a long tail or tippet hanging down from the top of the chaperon, or hood.   Originally liripipes were restricted to the head-coverings of the men, and especially of graduates.   In the latter form it still survives on the hood of the master of arts, etc.   But in the Middle Ages it was also worn depending from the top of the hood worn by all classes of men.   In time they were also affected in female costume. The chronicler Knighton describes women riding to tournaments, about the middle of the fourteenth century, wearing hoods and liripipes wrapped about their heads like cords.

From several illustrations of the costume of the humbler classes in the Louttrell Psalter, a fourteenth-century MS. in the British Museum, it appears that the caps worn were made of some woollen material, probably knitted so as to be capable of expanding to fit the head. These caps ended in a long narrow pipe, which in some cases hung down from the back of the head like a stocking. This apparently was the first form of the liripipe, which in the second half of the fifteenth century had developed into a kind of long band or fold extending from the back or top of the cap almost to the heels of the wearer; the sepulchral figures of William Canyuge, 1474, St. Mary's Church, Bristol (an effigy in the round), and a brass to a notary, *circa* 1475, at St. Mary Tower, Ipswich, are good typical examples. In both these cases the cap is of flat circular or turban form, and rests on the left shoulder, whilst the folded liripipe, consisting of a somewhat broad piece of material, falls downwards to the bottom of the tunic or gown, which at this period assumed a cassock-like appearance.

What may be regarded perhaps as a further, possibly the final, stage in the development of the liripipe is represented on a brass at Banwell Church, Somerset, to a civilian and wife, without inscription, but apparently of about the year 1480. In this brass the man is shown

with a kind of flat turban-like head-dress resting on his
right shoulder. Two strap-like attachments unite the
hanging scarf to the side of the head-dress, which has
a fur-covered rim. The scarf or "pipe" hangs, not
from the centre of the hat as before,
but is joined to the side of it, and joined
apparently in such a way as to be de-
tachable at pleasure.

It will be observed, from the examples already described, that the liripipe had assumed a length which may
well have been found, on occasions,
to be inconvenient, and it is only
reasonable to suppose that the straps
were added for the purpose of detach-
ing the hanging pipe when it was not
wanted.

In the monumental brass to Geoffrey
Kidwelly, Esquire, in Little Witten-
ham, Berkshire, who died in 1483, we
find a very similar arrangement. The
esquire is habited in civil costume, and
on his right shoulder is a flat turban-

Turban-like hat with like hat with a tassel on one side. The
scarf hanging there- pipe, which reaches considerably be-
from, *circa* 1480   low the knees, is suspended apparently
from the inside of the turban by means of two straps.
He also wears a fur-lined gown with girdle, from
which are suspended a pouch (or gypcière) and rosary.

A good example of the liripipe hanging as a flat
band or scarf from a turban-like hat which rests on

the left shoulder exists in the church of St. Mary the Virgin at Tenby. The effigy commemorates John White, Mayor of Tenby, and is of about the year 1490.

An excellent specimen of a liripipe hanging from a broad flat head-dress, and, like that, of black colour, occurs in the celebrated portrait of Edward Grimston preserved at Gorhambury. The picture bears the name of the artist, "Petrus Christi," the date when it was painted "1449," and the arms of Grimston, and is therefore one of the most interesting and ancient of English dated portraits.

For the present purpose, however, the chief value of the painting consists in the evidence it affords as to the dress of an English gentleman in the middle of the fifteenth century. As already hinted, the head-dress is perhaps the most striking garment represented. The hat, or bonnet, itself projects considerably all round, and from the centre of the crown, apparently, a broad black pipe or band falls down on the left-hand side of the wearer, being cut off a little above the waist, as the picture represents hardly a half-length view of the figure. A green sleeveless jacket is worn over a red tunic, and the latter, being open at the throat and chest, a white shirt of linen is shown below. The tunic is fastened in front by double bands, probably loops of red. A chain, perhaps of gold, hangs round the neck, and a collar of SS is held in the right hand.

MANTLE

The mantle was a very favourite form of outer garment with the ladies of the thirteenth, fourteenth, and fifteenth centuries. In form, in length, and in the disposition of its folds there are many varieties, but it is invariably a graceful garment and a pleasing addition to the figure.

In the celebrated Romsey effigy it appears to have been made of some fine material, falls gracefully from the shoulders, and is held up by the right hand, and also under the left arm. Its means of fastening is a loose cord or strap, which hangs as a festoon across the breast.

In an effigy to a member of the Warblington family, in Warblington Church, Hampshire, the mantle falls straight down from the shoulders, having no front fastening of any kind.

At Ryther Church, Yorkshire, is an early effigy of a lady wearing a mantle which is fastened by means of a flat strap or band fastened to both sides of the mantle a little above the breast by means of five foiled studs or bosses, probably of metal. The mantle is brought to the requisite tightness by manipulating the band.

The mantle of the effigy to a lady of the Clifford family in Worcester Cathedral is fastened by an ornamental brooch of gold made in diamond or quarry shape. A similar brooch in many ways, except that it is finer and more boldly designed, fastens the mantle in the effigy of the Lady Montacute (who died in 1354) at Oxford Cathedral. In the effigies of three of this lady's children the mantle fastenings present peculiarities. One (a lady) has her dark purple mantle lightly fastened across the breast by means of a chain of oblong links, each end of which is joined to a gold or gilt brooch or

ELIZABETH, WIFE OF LORD MONTACUTE,
(CIRCA 1354). OXFORD CATHEDRAL

possibly shield-shaped boss fixed in the mantle. A
son wears a magnificent crimson mantle fastened over
the right shoulder by means of four
flower-shaped brooches of square outline, whilst the front is decorated with
four circular brooches of metal, ornamented with a kind of concentric
circles. The edges of this fine mantle
are invected or scalloped, and its lining
is of blue material.

The mantle of Philippa of Hain-
ault, queen of King Edward III, who
died in 1369, according to the effigy
in Westminster Abbey, wore a thin
cord fastening to her mantle, the
diamond-shaped studs or brooches for
which were near the shoulders.

The usual method of fastening during the fifteenth century was by means
of a cord passing through loops at the
back of diamond-shaped studs and
brought down in front of the wearer
nearly to the waist, the cord ending
in two small tassels, and kept in
position by means of a slider. There
are many effigies—both those in the
round and also flat monumental
brasses—which illustrate these fastenings. (See HERALDIC MANTLES.)

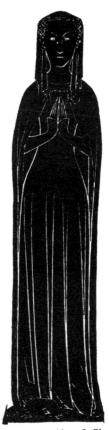

Eleanor, wife of Sir
Wm. de Burgate, 1409

PARTLET

The partlet was a covering of light material worn as a partial or complete screen for the neck and bosom of ladies at a period when dresses were cut low in front. The partlet is mentioned in inventories of the reign of Henry VIII as made of Venice gold knit, and also as made of white lawn wrought with gold.

Originally the partlet may have been a kerchief for the neck, and used by both sexes, but in the reign of Elizabeth, when low-cut dresses were much in vogue, it became the special property of the fair sex, and was in some cases richly ornamented with gold thread, pearls, stones, and jewels. Not infrequently it was shown open in front in order to display a necklace or pendent gem or jewel.

There does not appear to be any relation between the term partlet as applied to a piece of costume and the same word used of a favourite hen, of which two separate mentions are made by Shakespeare (*1 Henry IV*, III, 3, and *Winter's Tale*, II, 3).

ROSARY

The rosary was a chaplet of beads on which, as Dr. Johnson bluntly remarks, "the Romanists number their prayers." Judging from the representations of the rosary on monuments, it appears probable that the number of beads has varied at different times, but the rule was to divide the strand at every ten beads by one of larger size. At the recital of an ave a small bead was let fall from between the fingers, and so on, until a large bead was reached, when a paternoster was said. Usually a rosary contained five sets of ten small beads, divided by four larger beads and a cross.

It is an interesting fact that the wearing of the rosary was kept up longer by the men than by the women, and the custom seems to have been maintained longer in provincial and country districts than in London. The open use of the rosary ceased at the time of the religious disturbances in the sixteenth century.

SLEEVES (HANGING)

The various stages in the development of the pendent sleeves, which formed such a characteristic feature of the costumes of mediæval ladies, may be followed quite clearly in the series of sepulchral effigies engraved with extraordinary fidelity and beauty by Thomas and George Hollis.

The effigy to an unknown lady in Romsey Church, Hampshire, is the first of the series. The undermost visible garment is a gown reaching from the neck and wrists to the feet, where it falls in ample and graceful folds. Over this is a shorter garment which may be called the outer gown, a garment which reaches perhaps a little below the knees, and whose sleeves terminate about half-way between the wrist and the elbow. Above the elbow is a simple slit large enough for the arm to pass through. Over all is a mantle of fine material hanging in folds which is fastened across the breast by a

Rosary carried on the wrist, 1476

cord or thin strap. The interesting head-dress consisting of kerchief and bands is described in another
part of this volume (p. 145).

If the arm were brought through this slit the re-
mainder of the sleeve would hang down only a very
little way below the elbow. The date of this effigy
may be approximately placed at 1260.

The magnificent effigy of Elizabeth, wife of William
Lord Montacute, in Oxford Cathedral, is one of special
interest on account of the beautifully coloured robes
in which she is shown. She died in 1354, and on her
tomb are representations in effigy of her eight children.
One of them, the second figured on the plate in the
book referred to,[1] is a charming figure of a lady wearing a dark purple gown, over which is an outer gown
of pale blue colour reaching a little below the knees.
It is edged at the bottom with white, and its sleeves
terminate abruptly immediately above the elbow in a
white band which fits the arm closely. From this band
a white liripipe-like extension, too small for a sleeve,
falls from each elbow to a point somewhat below the
knees. This outer gown has nine or ten buttons extending from the neck to the middle, fastening up the
front of the garment as far as it is capable of being
opened, and there is a pocket slit set nearly perpendicularly on the right-hand side.

Another somewhat similar costume is found on the
effigy of one of the daughters of Edward III in
Westminster Abbey, the date of which is probably

[1] *The Monumental Effigies of Great Britain.* Drawn by T. and G.
Hollis.

1369. The points of difference are that the outer gown descends quite to the ground, is furnished with two quite perpendicular pockets, and has hanging from the arms long sleeve-like extensions which reach almost to the ground.

Still another example of this extravagant fashion of wearing very long hanging sleeves may be seen in the monumental brass to Sir John de la Pole and his wife Joan, *circa* 1370, at Chrishall, Essex. The lady's sleeves in this instance fall from the front of the elbows nearly to the feet.

The word liripipe has been used in describing sleeves of this type, but it may be questioned whether the use of such a term is wise. The liripipe seems to be more nearly related to the hood and the cap than to the sleeves.

Several fifteenth century brasses of ladies show them wearing an open mantle with dark lining, the result being that the strip of the outer side of the mantle shown often appears, in a heel-ball rubbing, to be a kind of hanging sleeve.

It is interesting to compare this fourteenth century fashion of hanging sleeves with that of the sixteenth century, when civilians, both male and female, are shown wearing very long sleeves pierced with a hole above the elbow for the convenience of passing the arm through them.

SMOCK

This is the old name for a woman's undermost garment, or chemise. It was anciently composed of the finest linen, and in the latter half of the thirteenth

century it had become the fashion to ornament the
material with embroidery in gold or coloured silk.
This fashion, which continued in vogue until the
middle of the seventeenth century, resembles that of
ornamenting the necks of the shirts worn by gentlemen during the sixteenth century, when elaborate embroidery in gold and colours, and even jewels, was
employed.

The smock-race, so popular at fairs and rural sports
during the eighteenth century, was a running contest
among village girls divested of every unnecessary
garment. The prize offered to the winner was a new
and ornamented smock.

STOMACHER

Although the stomacher was chiefly in vogue as an
article of ladies' attire in the reign of Queen Elizabeth,
and was worn particularly in association with the well-
developed farthingales prevalent in the latter part of
that reign, it was not limited to the time of Elizabeth,
nor was it used solely by the female sex. Towards the
end of the fifteenth century the stomacher was worn by
both sexes.

The prototype of the stomacher was perhaps the
placard or placate, a piece of dress worn by both men
and women from the time of Edward IV to that of
Henry VIII.

TREWS

These garments, from which our modern trousers
are evidently derived, are of very great antiquity in

this country.[1] The Celtic Druids ·were nicknamed "the long-trousered philosophers," and the Celts as a race were called the *Bracati*, or *Gentes Braccatæ*—"the trousered people."

The Romans in Britain wore the belted tunic, the toga, and the mantle, and it is from this type of garments that the Highland plaid and kilt are derived.

There are at Kilpech Church,[2] Herefordshire, some interesting carvings of Welsh knights whose costume includes trousers, or trews, close-fitting vests of rayed or striped materials, and caps with curved points of the kind generally known as Phrygian caps.

TROUSERS

This is perhaps the most important and certainly the chief distinguishing garment of the male sex among Europeans. It may be remarked that the use or non-use of this article of clothing has been adopted by some authorities as a criterion in classi-

Knight in trews (Kilpeck Church)

[1] An interesting article on the Celtic Trews is published in *The Scottish Historical Review*, Vol. I, pp. 389–98.

[2] See *Archæologia*, Vol. XXX, pp. 62–3.

fying the men of the great human family throughout the world. "The nations of the ancient world," says one writer, "might be fairly divided into two great groups or classes—the trousered and the untrousered. Amongst the latter were the Greeks and Romans, deriving their origin, as it appears to be generally acknowledged, from the bare-legged Egyptians; while two great branches of the Scythic or Northern Asiatic family, which had overrun Europe, and colonized the South of Britain long previous to the Roman invasion, viz. the Kimmerii and the Kelte, wore the distinguishing close trousers or loose pantaloons."

Notwithstanding the very general custom in the present time of wearing trousers in England, it is a curious fact that whilst the inhabitants of Scotland and Ireland derive their custom of wearing that garment from a remote period of antiquity, and with almost uninterrupted continuity, the English custom is of comparatively recent origin. In the form of breeches fitting closely to the limbs these garments were worn in the time of Henry VIII, whilst in the reign of Queen Elizabeth garments known by the somewhat similar name of "trossers," but made of a looser cut, were in fashion. In one of Ben Jonson's plays a character is described as walking "in his gowne, waistecoate and *trouses*."

The word trousers has been considered by some authorities to have been derived from the verb to truss, i.e. to tuck up or fasten the hose by points to the doublet, but others suppose it to have been taken from trews of ancient times. (See TREWS.)

The modern trousers have clearly grown out of the breeches which were so universally worn during the Stuart period. Towards the middle of the seventeenth century the length of the breeches was considerably increased, as is shown by certain contemporary evidence.

A writer in one of the London newspapers, in 1762, complains that "The mode-makers of the age have taken an antipathy to the leg, for by their high-topped shoes and long trouser-like breeches with a broad kneeband, like a compress for the rotula, a leg in high taste is not longer than a Common Councilman's tobacco stopper."

In the reign of George II it was the fashion to have trousers made of black velvet, and during the eighteenth century, and a few years beyond it, it was a very usual thing to have these garments made of various brightly coloured cloths. In the latter half of the eighteenth century doe or buckskin breeches were much worn by gentlemen, even for walking dress, and it was considered to be the height of fashion to have them made so tight that the most extraordinary means had to be used for getting into them.

In some of the exaggerated fashions of modern trousers, notably in those varieties affected by the British seaman and the London "coster"—there appears to be a tendency to "throw back" to the baggy or pantaloon type, but, generally speaking, the garment is very constant in form, material, and colour.

VEIL

This was a very important part of a lady's costume
during the reign of Elizabeth. It was composed of
very thin material, and cannot ever have been of much
practical utility. Its purpose was purely ornamental,
and special means were taken to render it suitable and
effectual. In several of Elizabeth's portraits we find
the veil is made to assume wing-like forms by means
of stiffenings of wire, and the effect is sometimes
heightened by edgings of pearls and even jewels. In
other portraits, mostly those of the earlier part of
Elizabeth's reign, the veil descends from the head
downwards in such a way as to partly cover the
shoulders.

The fan, formed of ostrich feathers and furnished
with a richly jewelled handle, was usually carried as
part of the costume when the winged veils were in
vogue.

VEST

From what has been said of the origin of the coat,
it is not difficult to make out the origin and growth of
the modern vest or waistcoat. The latter name indicates
the main purpose of the garment, namely, a closely
fitting article of clothing to be worn round the chest
and waist. When the vest of the seventeenth century
grew to the dimensions of a coat, the waistcoat was
introduced (as a garment tightly fitting around the
body) to supply the deficiency. In the seventeenth
and eighteenth centuries the vest seems to have been
generally of a gorgeous and richly ornamented char-

acter, and in the period extending from the first years of the present century to past the year 1851 coloured vests, often of brilliant hues, were by no means uncommon. Figured and flowered satin vests were perhaps the most correct thing for gentlemen fifty years ago.

WIDOWS' WEEDS

The wearing of a distinctive costume to denote widowhood is a very ancient fashion, and in England at any rate it seems always to have taken more or less the same form. The chief garments which distinguish widows from other ladies are the barbe, which is usually drawn up close under the chin, the long kerchief over the head, and the capacious, mantle-like cloak. These, it will be noted, are garments similar to those worn by nuns, and there is reason to believe that the flowing kerchief drawn over the head was the origin of the modern "widow's weeds."

The relation between widowed ladies and nuns was rather close, and the matter is one which requires a short explanation. The position of a wealthy widow in the Middle Ages must have been one of peculiar difficulty. One can quite conceive that the attentions of unwelcome suitors, to say nothing of the powerful and unruly barons, must have made seclusion in a monastic house on the part of the widow who possessed a valuable estate a desirable, if not an absolutely necessary, step. Hence arose an order of vowesses, widows who, either from pious or prudent motives, withdrew themselves from the world and assumed a monastic garb. These ladies took a vow of

chastity, and in token thereof donned veil head-dress
and plaited barbe or gorget, wearing the latter above or
below the chin according to their higher or lower rank
in life.

When a lady took the vow of chastity after the death

Head-dress of widow, *circa* 1460

of her husband she was called a vowess.   Canon
Raine, in *Testamenta Eboracensin*, Vol. III, page
312,[1] points out that a kind of investiture took place,
generally during or before a celebration of the Mass,
when the officiating bishop, abbot, or prior, gave the

[1] Surtees Society's Publications, No. 45 (1864).

vowess a pall or mantle, a veil and a ring, and she then made a vow of chastity in a form of set words. This vow, which was made in the presence of several witnesses, obliged the lady to live in chastity. She was not severed from the world, but could live in it and make a will, and dispose of her property as she chose. Sometimes a vowess, for the sake of a stricter and more retired life, took up her abode in or near some monastic house, particularly a nunnery, but she did not become a regular nun, remaining rather in the position of a lodger.

A widow lady, about 1440 (Stoke Dabernon, Surrey)

In the work referred to the text is given of several vows taken by ladies who were widows. These range from 1374 to 1400, and are variously in Latin, French, and English. Further information on this interesting subject will be found in a valuable contribution by the late Mr. J. L. André, F.S.A., to the *Archæological Journal* (Vol. XLIX, pp. 69–82), entitled "Widows and Vowesses."

Norfolk contains two undoubted monuments to vowesses, namely that to Juliana Angell, about the year 1500, at Witton Church, near Blofield, and another to Joan Braham, 1519, at Frenze, a small church in Norfolk. In the former example the garments worn are gown, mantle, barbe or gorget, and veil, all quite plain in character; and in the latter, gown, barbe, veil, and a mantle furnished with cords which end in tassels, whilst the gown is confined by an ornamental girdle and has cuffs. No ring is seen on either figure. It may be gathered from this that it is by no means easy to distinguish between widows who were and widows who were not vowesses.

WIMPLE

The wimple was a favourite article of feminine attire, worn as a covering for the head and chin. Wimple is another name for the veil or kerchief, although in Chaucer's line in the *Romaunt of the Rose*,

" Weryng a fayle in-stide of wymple,"

we have an indication that in the fourteenth century there was a distinction between them. The same writer in another place speaks of nuns wearing veils and wimples, from which it may be inferred that the wimple was the part of the garment which covered the chin, throat, and breast, whilst the veil was that which covered the head.

The wimple, which was worn by ladies from Anglo-Saxon times down to the middle of the sixteenth century, was essentially an article of clothing intended to veil female charms. Modest women were, as Chaucer puts it, " gwimpled well."

The wimple, besides being a garment generally worn by ladies, was also, and still is, essentially a part of the conventual dress of nuns.

The natural effect of the general use of the wimple is that jewellery in the form of chains round the neck, etc., is hidden in the sepulchral effigies and brasses representing ladies, and thus what would have been valuable evidence of the prevalent fashion in ladies' ornaments during the Middle Ages is not available.

CHAPTER XI

MILITARY COSTUME

ARMOUR

THE earliest kinds of military costume of which
we have definite traces were largely of a defensive character.   Weapons of offence of an antiquity as great as the Neolithic Period have been found
in abundance in this country, but no sufficient evidence
has been found to enable one to ascertain precisely, or
even approximately, what means of defence were employed against the flint-pointed arrows, lances, or
spears, or the heavy stone axes of those early times.

In the Bronze Age we have proofs of the use of
circular shields or bucklers of bronze ; but these, of
course, are of the nature of defensive arms rather than
armour as a covering for the body.

The early Iron Age furnishes us with practically
no evidence as to the military clothing or armour
in use at that time, but we know from actual
remains of swords, spears, etc., which have been preserved that the weapons of offence were of formidable
character, and we may assume that defensive armour
was correspondingly developed.

When we arrive at the Roman period, however, the
case is different, and if we have few remaining traces of

the actual armour now left, we have abundant proof of
its use, as well as its forms and methods of construction, in statuary and other forms of ancient art.

The Roman soldiers were well protected by defensive
armour. The foot soldier wore a laminated cuirass or
lorica, consisting of bands of brass about three inches
wide extending about half round the body, and
fastened upon a leathern or quilted ground-work.
Below this, and reaching hardly as low as the knees,
he wore a tunic, whilst the legs were covered by tight
drawers which descended to the level of the calf.
Sometimes the tunic was covered with leather or felt
straps, four or five inches long, and protected by plates
of metal. Another type of body-defence for the Roman
foot soldier consisted of scale armour, formed of plates
of steel or gilded bronze fastened upon a substructure
of leather. Helmets and military sandals, called *caligæ*,
were also in use, and a belt for suspension of dagger
or short sword was worn diagonally over the left
shoulder and under the right arm.

Britain has not furnished many actual remains of
Roman armour, although some important and remarkable pieces, including about 350 bronze scales from a
cuirass, have lately been unearthed at the Roman camp
at Newstead, in Scotland, and others have been found
at Ham Hill, Somerset ; but a good many pieces of
statuary, as well as mosaic pavements, found on
Roman sites, afford valuable representations of the
forms of armour in vogue.

At Housesteads (Borcovicus), on the great Roman
Wall of Hadrian, several good pieces of sculpture have

been found. Some among them portray soldiers clothed in tunics, the lower part of which is defended by scale armour. The sword, in some cases, is carried on the left-hand side, but in others, especially when the weapon is short, it is carried on the right-hand side. In one case a Roman soldier dressed in civil dress is represented. He wears a tunic and mantle, the latter being gracefully suspended from the left arm. This mantle is fastened by a fibula over the right shoulder, leaving the sword-arm free. The garment is decorated with a fringed edging three inches deep. This species of decoration, as we learn from C. Roach Smith's *Collectanea Antiqua* (Vol. III, p. 81), was much used in Romano-Gaulish costume.

There are but scanty traces of armour of the Anglo-Saxons. Helmets, composed of ribs of iron radiating from the crown of the head and covered with horn or leather, appear to have been in use. One such, or rather remains of one, were dug up at Leckhampton Hill, near Cheltenham, and in association with it was a mass of iron chainwork, formed of large numbers of links, of two descriptions, attached to each other by small rings, half an inch in diameter. Traces of cloth were also found over the surface of these iron rings, and the probability is that the whole deposit represented a mass of partially decayed body-armour composed of a kind of chain-mail.

Before the time of the Norman Conquest, English costume and armour had become much modified by Norman influence. Evidence of this is not wanting in the armour shown in the Bayeux Tapestry. Thus,

Count Guy wears a tunic of what is apparently scale-armour under his mantle. In another scene, that in which Duke William gives arms to Harold (that is, arms him after a knightly manner), both are clothed in defensive garments resembling chain mail, which cover the entire body, the arms, and the legs down to the knees. William appears to wear leg-coverings of a banded nature which fit pretty closely.

The details of the needlework of this interesting work are not sufficiently precise to enable us to form any certain idea of the nature of these pieces of body armour, but in a subsequent scene depicting William's men carrying wine and other stores on board the ships, four of these hauberk-like articles are well shown, being carried by means of poles thrust through the arm-holes, a circumstance of twofold interest for our purpose, (1) as indicating the exact shape of the garment, and (2) as suggesting considerable weight, such, indeed, as one might expect if iron chain mail were employed.

When about to mount his horse and go out to give battle to Harold, William appears enveloped in a hauberk reaching to the knees where it terminates in a broad band, in closely fitting leg-coverings, and in a conically shaped hat. The last, presumably, is of iron; the other coverings are apparently of chain-mail in which circular rings as well as a kind of lattice ground-work are well shown in the needlework. William appears similarly armed when he is represented on horseback and conversing with his chief military officer, Vital. It is noteworthy that whilst these two have mail coverings for the legs the rest of the armed knights do not possess them.

In these pictures, as well as in others representing the actual conflict, it is easy to see that the hauberk or shirt of mail was so shaped as to cover the head, leaving the face bare. Conical iron hats or helmets with well-developed nose-guards afforded additional protection for the head.

The armour worn during the time of Henry I or Stephen consisted, according to the evidence of a British Museum MS.,[1] of a hauberk of mail which enveloped the head, body, and arms, and fell as a short skirt down to the knees ; a helmet with nasal guard and pointed crown ; and high boots reaching half-way between the foot and the knee, and leaving the rest of the legs unprotected. Another species of hauberk worn at this time was open at the sides up to the hips.

The armour of the latter part of the thirteenth century and of the fourteenth and fifteenth centuries is so well depicted on the effigies on monumental brasses and sepulchral effigies that we can hardly find a better series of illustrations to show its various changes. Before calling attention to the more important points, however, it may be useful to give a brief description of the different parts of the arms and armour of the period under the names by which the parts were known.

[1] Cotton. MS., Nero, C, 4.

AILETTES

Defensive ornaments of various shapes worn on the shoulders as little wings. They were introduced as part of the armour of English knights towards the close of the thirteenth century, but belong mainly to the reign of Henry II (1307-1327).

BAINBERGS

Shin-guards of leather or iron, strapped over the chausses of mail, as additional defences to the front of the legs. Bainbergs were the precursors of the steel greaves or jambes of the fourteenth century.

BASCINET

A light helmet worn like a skull-cap, worn with or without a movable front. They belong mainly to the thirteenth and fourteenth centuries.

BASILARD

A weapon very generally worn by civilians during the Middle Ages. It was longer than the anelace. The latter was a stabbing weapon, but the basilard was for cutting.

BAUDRICK OR BALDRICK

A belt of leather and often richly ornamented, worn diagonally across the body from the shoulders to the waist, from which the sword was suspended.

BESAGUES OR MOTONS

Small plates of mail worn in the fourteenth and fifteenth centuries as defences for the armpits or

shoulders.   (See an important article on the subject by
Viscount Dillon, v.p.s.a., in *The Archæological Journal*,
Vol. LXIV, pp. 15–23.)

BRASSARTS

Plate armour of several pieces for the upper part of
the arm, sometimes in a single piece of plate. (See
REREBRACES.)

BREASTPLATE OR CUIRASS

Armour for the breast and back.

CAMAIL

Chain mail protection for the neck and shoulders,
attached to the bascinet when that head-piece was introduced in the fourteenth century.

CHAUSSES

Tight, armed coverings of mail for the legs and feet.
They were laced behind the leg.

COIF DE MAILLES

The hood-like covering of chain mail in which the
head was enclosed.   The chin and all except the face
was covered by this coif.   Under it, as under all chain
mail, padded defences were worn.

CUISSES

Pieces of armour for the protection of the thighs.

CYCLAS OR CICLATOUN

These terms implied (1) a lady's gown and (2) a
short gown worn by knights.   In the latter sense it

succeeded the surcoat. Thus Sir John d'Aubernoun, who died in 1277, is represented as wearing the surcoat, whilst his son of the same name, who died in 1327, wears the cyclas. The cyclas is not so long in front as the surcoat, being cut short in front for convenience when riding. The name was doubtless given in allusion to the rich material of which it was composed.

ELBOW-COPS

Elbow-pieces of plate, which first appear in the mixed armour of the latter half of the thirteenth century.

FALD, SKIRT OR PETTICOAT OF MAIL

This was worn beneath the tuilles, and generally descended lower than them.

GAMBESON. (SEE JUPON)

GAUNTLETS

These defensive coverings for the hands were introduced during the reign of Edward I, taking the place of the ends of the hauberk, which had formerly been made long enough to cover the tips of the fingers. Some gauntlets were only of leather, but others were covered with scales and sometimes spiked plates of steel. It is noteworthy that when composite sword-hilts came in gauntlets went out of use.

GORGET OR STANDARD OF PLATE

An armed defence for the neck, much worn by the soldiers of Queen Elizabeth.

GREAVES

Armour for the legs.   (See BAINBERGS.)

HABERGEON

This was a coat of mail or a breast-plate, lighter and shorter than the hauberk, of which it may be regarded as a diminutive.

HAKETON

A tunic of leather, buckram, etc., stuffed with wool or tow, and stitched in parallel lines.   It was worn beneath the hauberk so as to diminish the weight of the chain mail, and was really much the same as the gambeson.

HAUBERK

This interesting and important piece of armour, it is believed, was originally intended for the defence of the neck and shoulders, but by the thirteenth century it had been developed into a long coat of mail or military tunic, usually of chain mail, which was pliant and easily accommodated itself to the bodily movements of the wearer.   The following are some of the variations of the word : halsberg, halsberga, halberc, halbergium, alsbergium, haubercum, and haubert.

JUPON, GIPON, OR GYPELL

This was a close-fitting vest, tunic, or doublet, especially one worn by knights under the hauberk. It was sometimes made of thick stuff and padded.   It is believed to have been identical with the gambeson, which was afterwards, if quilted, called the pourpoint. Originally this garment was worn under the armour, but later on it was faced with rich materials and embroidered, when it was worn without armour. Chaucer speaks of the "jupoun" being composed of fustian, and stained by having been in contact with the "haburgeoun." (See HABERGEON.)

KNEE-COPS OR POLEYNS

The common name for these defensive coverings for the knees was knee-cops. The material was either boiled leather or metal, and in the thirteenth and fourteenth centuries they were richly ornamented.

MISERICORDE. (SEE BASILARD)

PASGUARDS

Additional pieces of plate armour, attached to the elbow-cops or elbow-pieces.

PAULDRONS

Defensive plates of armour for the shoulders. They and the brassarts were composed of several successive plates.

PLACCATES

Two or more pieces of which the armour for the breast was composed. They were made to overlap, so as to impart some amount of flexibility to the armour. The lower one was called a pance.

The term has many variations, such as placcards, demi-placcates, etc.

REREBRACES

Armour for the defence of the parts of the arm above the elbow. (See VAMBRACES.)

ROUNDELS

Small circular shields used in the thirteenth and fourteenth centuries.

SOLLERETS

These were the defensive coverings for the feet, and consisted of a number of overlapping plates so arranged that they would bend with every movement of the foot. There is a good paper on the subject by James James, F.S.A., in the *Journal of the Archæological Association*, Vol. XI.

SPURS

These well-known objects were of two types. The first, known as the " pryck-spur," had simply a single goad or point with or without a neck ; the other type had a rowel, a kind of wheel with a number of points. These are first seen on the great seals of Henry III.

STANDARD OF MAIL

A species of collar of mail, designed to protect the throat of the wearer. An improvement upon this form was introduced in or about the year 1400, when the mail collar was superseded by a gorget, or standard of plate.

SURCOAT

A garment worn by both sexes in the thirteenth and fourteenth centuries. It was, however, specially characteristic of the armour of knights during the twelfth and thirteenth centuries, giving place to the cyclas early in the fourteenth century.

TABARD

The heraldic surcoat of a herald or knight. A jacket or sleeveless coat.

TACES, OR TASSETS

Flexible bands of steel surrounding the hips. They extended from the waist to the middle of the thigh, and consisted of from four to eight separate bands.

TILTING HELM

The large, heavy helmet entirely covering the head and face, used by those engaged in tilting, etc., as a protection against the lance of the opponent.

TUILLES

Extra pieces of plate armour in the form of guards hanging from the taces.

VAMBRACES

Defensive armour for the forearm, extending from the elbow to the wrist.

THIRTEENTH CENTURY

The effigy at Bitton, Gloucestershire, probably commemorating Sir Walter de Bitton (father of Thomas de Bitton, Bishop of Exeter 1293–1307), who died in 1227, admirably illustrates the armour of his time. He is protected in a complete suit of banded mail, and bears on the breast his sword diagonally placed, and a large shield bearing his arms, *ermine, a fess gules*. He is crossed-legged, and wears a surcoat. The monument was discovered in the churchyard at Bitton.

One thirteenth century monumental brass, which happens to be the earliest now existing in the kingdom,

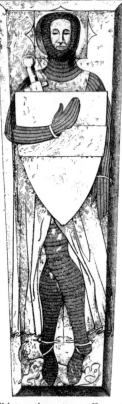

may be mentioned here on account of its extraordinary interest both as a piece of fine metal-engraving and as a picture of the military equipment or "harness" of a knight in the last quarter of the thirteenth century. The memorial is that of Sir John d'Aubernoun, died 1277, which still remains in the church of Stoke Dabernon, Surrey.

The effigy may be unhesitatingly placed within the "surcoat" period, as it consists almost entirely of chain mail covered to some extent by a garment of that character. It is a curious fact, to which the late Mr. J. G. Waller, F.S.A., drew attention about half a century ago,[1] that this is the only effigy of the time of Edward I that has not the legs crossed. This is interesting, but the idea that knights with crossed legs had rendered military service in the Holy Land, or were

Thirteenth century effigy of knight, probably Sir Walter de Bitton (Bitton Church, Gloucestershire)

[1] *Monumental Brasses from the Thirteenth to the Sixteenth Century.* Mr. Waller's description of the armour has been closely followed in reference to this and some other of the thirteenth and fourteenth century military effigies.

Effigy to Sir John d'Aubernoun, 1277 (Stoke Dabernon, Surrey)

under a vow to do so, has long been exploded, although that view was commonly held some years ago.

The figure is entirely enveloped in a suit of interlaced chain mail, the body being covered by a hauberk with sleeves; the head is protected by a hood or coif of mail which is drawn over it; the legs and feet are guarded by chausses; at the knees are coverings of plate ornamented with roses; and the spurs are of the simple "prick-spur" type. The surcoat, just referred to, is loose, and has a fringed border; it is confined at the waist by a plaited cord, below which it opens in front and falls on either side in ample folds. An enriched guige passing over the right shoulder supports on the opposite side a heater-shaped shield, emblazoned with armorial bearings; the ornament on the guige consists alternately of a rose slipped, and a fylfot within a lozenge space placed in a square. The sword is suspended by a broad, slightly ornamental belt. The scabbard is plain; the pommel of the sword is curiously worked with a cross in the centre. A lance passes under the right arm, the shaft resting on the ground. This lance, at a point just below the head of the knight, bears a pennon charged with the Aubernoun arms. The feet rest on a lion couchant, which holds the bottom of the lance between his paws, and grasps the staff with his teeth.

On close scrutiny certain defects will be observed in the drawing of the figure, but as a production of the burin, this brass is not excelled by any later example. Each link of the mail is distinctly represented, and the mere work of engraving such a large surface must have occupied many weeks, if not months, of patient labour.

The effigy of Sir Roger de Trumpington in Trumpington Church, near Cambridge, is a work of the year 1289, or thereabouts. The engraving of the brass is unfinished, but quite enough was executed to show the general features of the armour, the character of which closely resembles that of the last-named effigy. The points of difference are that the Trumpington effigy is shown furnished with oblong wing-like plates, or ailettes, at the back of the shoulders, whilst the head is resting on a large helm, features which are not found on the D'Aubernoun brass. The ailettes, which made their appearance during the reign of Edward I and remained in fashion until that of Edward III, are curious additions to the armour, the purpose of which is not at present quite clear. It is probable that they were composed mainly of leather. They were sometimes fringed at the margin, and had badges and other designs, whilst the surface was covered with arms. The form of ailettes was usually square or oblong, but round, pentagonal, and lozenge shapes have been recorded.[1]

FOURTEENTH CENTURY

The monumental brass to Sir Robert Bures at Acton Church, Suffolk, comes just into the fourteenth century, the date being about the year 1302. This effigy is a superb piece of work, the drawing of the figure and

[1] Fairholt's *Costume in England*. Edited by Hon. H. F. Dillon. II, 5.

the execution of the engraving being both of great
merit. There is not much change to note from the
armour of the two preceding effigies, but the ornamentation is more delicate and richer,
particularly on the pieces which protect the knees. These are known
as knee-cops, and they appear to
have been made either of boiled
leather (*cuir bouilli*) or plates of
steel. The extraordinary richness
of ornament which they bear may
be seen from the accompanying
illustration.

Knee-cops and Cuis-
ses, from the brass to
Robert de Bures, 1302
(Acton, Suffolk)

The monumental brass to Sir
Robert de Septvans, at Chartham
Church, Kent, brings us to another
stage in the development of the
ornament rather than that of the actual character of
defensive armour. The scabbard of the sword and
the sword-belt are enriched throughout; the ailettes
are set at an angle behind the shoulders; and the
head and hands are freed from the chain mail which
falls down of its own weight. But the chief points for
notice are (1) the arms embroidered on the surcoat
and (2) the appearance beneath the gambeson of the
quilted garment, known as the haketon. A similar
material passes over the knee, forming a pad for the
knee-cops. The date of the figure can be placed with
some certainty at about the year 1306.

The effigy to a knight belonging to the Bacon family
at Gorleston, Suffolk, furnishes a good example of the

armour of about the year 1320. The effigy, which is defective, is cross-legged, and is shown as encased

Effigy to a member of the Bacon family, about the year 1320 (Gorleston, Suffolk)

in banded mail, and furnished with ailettes, placed lozenge-wise, and charged with a cross. This is an excellent example of the end of the surcoat period.

It is hardly necessary to add, after what has been said, that the cross-legged attitude of the knight has no relation to the Crusades. It was a simple and convenient method of indicating the repose of the recumbent body.

An interesting although somewhat damaged effigy of an armed knight of what is known as the cyclas period (1325–30) is in St. Peter's Church, Sandwich, Kent. The effigy, which is of Caen stone, was formerly painted. It represents the knight wearing a quilted gambeson. Upon that is a hauberk of chain mail, then a defence of scale-work, and over all a fringed sleeveless surcoat or cyclas. On the arm is seen a portion of the gambeson, and above it is

Sculptured effigy of a Knight of the fourteenth century
in St. Peter's Church, Sandwich, Kent

HEAD OF THE EFFIGY OF EDWARD THE BLACK PRINCE IN CANTERBURY
CATHEDRAL

PART OF EFFIGY (SHOWING BELT AND SURCOAT WITH ROYAL ARMS)
OF EDWARD THE BLACK PRINCE, CANTERBURY CATHEDRAL

the loose sleeve of the hauberk, furnished with roundels at elbows and shoulder. The bascinet is round. The helm is attached by means of a chain to the lion-mask on the cyclas. The dagger hilt is also secured by a chain, while a cord suspends the sheath.

The effigy is now in the west end of the church, and has sustained a good deal of damage, but originally it must have been a splendid illustration of a knight of the earlier part of the fourteenth century. Similar but complete effigies exist at Horley and Folkestone.

The effigy of Sir John d'Aubernoun the second, who died in 1327, wears the cyclas, an outer garment which fits the figure more closely than the surcoat, and is considerably shorter in front than behind. It will be noticed that the hauberk is shaped almost to a point in front. On the head is a pointed bascinet, and from it hangs the camail or chain armour defence for the throat, neck, and shoulders.

On comparing this effigy with that of the earlier knight, Sir John d'Aubernoun, who died just fifty years before, we see a remarkable development of plate mail, which was now rapidly replacing chain mail.

By the middle of the fourteenth century, or soon after, we find that the legs and arms are entirely encased in plate armour. The head was protected by the bascinet; the throat by the camail and sometimes the standard of mail; and the feet by sollerets provided with overlapping plates riveted together. The effigy of Edward the Black Prince in Canterbury Cathedral belongs to this century. The prince died in 1376, and the effigy, which is represented in armour, may be considered artistically one of the very finest specimens in existence. As will be seen from the illustrations, it possesses a magnificent orle round the

head, and a superb belt and surcoat or tabard embroidered with the royal arms. In certain minute points, however, such as the fastenings and hinges of the armour, the effigy, which is a casting in bronze, is defective; but the general form is extremely good.

FIFTEENTH AND SIXTEENTH CENTURIES

Quite early in the fifteenth century complete plate armour began to be used, and of this species of defence monumental brasses and effigies in the round furnish us with abundant illustrations.

An example of the armour worn about the middle of the sixteenth century is here shown. The general awkwardness of the figure, it may be remarked, is due to the lack of skill of the artist who depicted it,

Armed knight, 1409 (Sir William de Burgate, at Burgate Church, Suffolk) but, in addition to this obvious defect, there is abundant evidence of deterioration in the various parts of the armour. One of the characteristic pieces of the time is the skirt or

i FOOT. UTTING Sc

Effigy of Sir John d'Aubernoun, 1327 (Stoke Dabernon, Surrey)

petticoat of mail usually worn under the tuilles, but there are one or two cases on record of the tuilles being beneath the mail skirt. The protective coverings for

Effigy to Sir Robert Suckling, of about the year 1415 (Barsham, Suffolk)

Sir Thomas Throckmorton, 1445 (Fladbury, Worcestershire)

P

the feet, the broad-toed sabbatons, are singularly clumsy.

The breast-plates of this period are generally with-

Esquire in armour, 1512
(Robert Whyte, in South Warnborough Church, Hants)

out placcates and have the perpendicular ridge, known as the tapul, down the centre.

A curious but interesting effigy of an armed figure of the year 1512 exists in a monumental brass at South

Warnborough Church, Hampshire. The figure is
represented as kneeling with the right knee on his
sword, which, with his gauntlets, have been discarded
and lie on the ground. The angularity of the armour
is remarkable.

Christopher Lytkott, Esq., 1554   Robert Rampston, 1585
(Swallowfield, Berks)

The costume worn by the members of the sovereign's
bodyguard, popularly called the "Yeomen of the
Guard," is shown in the effigy of Robert Rampston,
1586, formerly at Chingford, Essex (see engraving).
The tunic, which is quite short, has embroidered on

the breast a large figure of a rose surmounted by a crown. A ruff at the neck, breeches reaching just below the knees, tight nether-hose, and shoes complete the attire.

The rise and decline of armour are traceable to a regular series of circumstances. The development of really serviceable swords, lances, and battleaxes had the natural effect of increasing the means of defence such as helms, helmets, and coverings for the body made of scale, mail or plate armour. When gunpowder was introduced, and improved firearms made armour no longer effective, armour went out of fashion.

MILITARY UNIFORM

When armour as a means of bodily defence was abandoned, its place was not immediately taken by a set of clothing, or "uniform" as it has come to be called ; and materials for the study are, if not exactly scanty, scarcely as clear as might be wished.

The types of armour were subject to change and development to meet the requirements of new methods and implements of warfare, and to some extent they followed new fancies and fashions imported from France or other parts of the Continent. Yet all these changes had definite sequence, and can be referred without hesitation to restricted periods.

When armour ceased to be largely worn, and the soldiers were dressed in garments whose primary use was to protect them from the natural elements rather than human antagonists, we look in vain for the same persistence of form and regular sequence of fashion.

Soldier of the time of Charles I, armed with musket and sword,
carrying musket-rest, and with bandolier over the shoulder

When the Civil Wars began between the Parliament and King Charles I the soldiers of both armies were dressed in whatever colours their colonels chose to select.

At Edgehill [writes Professor Firth[1]] every variety of hue was visible on the backs of Essex's army. The regiments of Denzil Holles and Lord Robartes had red coats, Lord Brooke's regiment purple coats, Lord Saye's blue, Colonel Ballard's grey, Colonel Hampden's green. Amongst the ranks of the Royalists there was the same diversity of tint. In that battle the two sides were distinguished simply by the fact that Essex's men wore orange scarves and those of the King red. In the absence of these scarves it was impossible to determine whether a man belonged to one army or the other. At Marston Moor when Sir Thomas Fairfax, in consequence of the defeat of the cavalry he commanded, found himself alone amongst the enemy, he took the white handkerchief out of his hat (which was the sign of the Parliamentarians that day) and passed through for one of their own commanders, till he reached Cromwell's victorious troops.

Several other incidents could be given to show that in the early part of the war military uniform was irregular.

In the year 1645, however, the whole army under Sir Thomas Fairfax was dressed in red, and from that time onwards to the present day red has remained the predominant colour in English military uniform. As Fairfax's own colours were blue, his regiment had blue facings. The Protector Richard Cromwell gave all the foot soldiers about London new red coats

_____
[1] *Cromwell's Army*, pp. 232-3.

trimmed with black to wear at his father's funeral in
November, 1658.

The various parts of a soldier's clothing in 1642, as
we learn from certain contracts for the army in Ulster,
were: a cap, a doublet, a cassock or coat, breeches, two
pair of stockings, two pair of shoes, and two shirts.

There are in Ogilby's book[1] many interesting details
of military uniform, including those of the Yeomen of
the Guard, footmen, pages, etc., represented as attend-
ing Charles II on the occasion of his coronation. The
uniform of the yeomen is of special interest from the
fact that it still bears a close resemblance to the military
garb worn close upon four centuries ago. Their dress
is mentioned in 1513, when Henry VIII was attended
by six hundred archers of his guard all in white gab-
erdines and caps ; but there is reason to think that it
was not until the year 1526 that a distinctive costume
was appropriated to them.

In Charles II's time the present dress of the Yeomen
of the Guard was worn with the long skirts supersed-
ing the short "livery coat," as seen in the Cowdray
picture, *temp.* H. VIII.

The Yeomen of the Guard wore a scarlet habit,
guarded and laced on the skirts and sleeves with
garter blue velvet, and on their breasts and backs is
the Union rose ensigned with the crown royal embroidered with gold. The rose was combined with the
thistle after the accession of James I, and the shamrock
was added in 1802, after the union with Ireland.

[1] *The Entertainment of Charles II in his Passage through the City of
London to his Coronation.* 1662.

SOLDIER OF THE TIME OF JAMES I, ARMED WITH A CALIVER

There is at East Wickham, Kent, a monumental brass representing " William Payne, late Youman of the Guarde," who died in 1568. He is clothed in doublet and trunk hose, with rose and crown on the breast. The sleeves are puffed at the shoulder, and overlapped by a kind of epaulet. He wears a ruff round the neck, and carries a sword by his side.

Yeomen of the Guard wore scarlet hose up to the reign of George II. Subsequently blue, grey, and white were worn ; but finally red hose, with the ruffs of Elizabeth's time, were restored by George IV.

The soldiers of the time of James I were chiefly pikemen and musketeers, both of whom continued to wear metal head-pieces, whilst the pikemen wore thin corselets and carried a very formidable weapon in the form of a spear, in some cases eighteen feet long. He also wore a short sword. The musketeer's chief weapon was a musket, a heavy firearm which required to be supported upon a rest when it was fired. Charges of powder sufficient for each firing were contained in a number of small covered receptacles supported from a bandolier or leathern belt slung over the shoulder.

In the middle of the eighteenth century the most characteristic part of military uniform was the tall, mitre-like head-piece, or sugar-loaf cap, worn by the grenadiers, a feature which has been represented again and again in engravings and pictures of the period. Evelyn mentions this head-dress under the year 1678. A good example of the actual head-piece is preserved in the Victoria and Albert Museum.

Fairholt, in his *Costume in England* (Vol. I, p. 379,

1885 edition), figures a soldier and a sailor of the year
1746.   The sailor wears a small flat cocked hat; an
open jacket, displaying his shirt, the collar being turned
over on his shoulders; and loose slops similar to the
petticoat breeches of the reign of Charles II, and which
are still seen on Dutch soldiers, as well as upon some
of our own fishermen.

The soldier, one of the foot guards, wears a cocked
hat, a long skirted tunic, knee-breeches, and buttoned-
up gaiters.   The front of the tunic is thrown back and
decorated with laced button-holes.   The ammunition
bag hangs from a broad band or strap passing over the
left shoulder.

Armour may be considered to have been entirely
abandoned in the time of Queen Anne, when the pike,
as a fighting weapon, went out of fashion.   At this
time the red and white feather appeared in the hat.
The white cockade was adopted by the followers of the
Pretender, and the soldiers of George II wore, as a
distinguishing mark, a black cockade.

It may be added that the Household Cavalry first
wore cuirasses at the coronation of George IV.

CHAPTER XII

ECCLESIASTICAL COSTUME

ECCLESIOLOGICAL authorities are not in entire agreement as to the origin and early development of some of the ecclesiastical vestments used in England. Indeed, some of the points of difference have been at times discussed with considerable warmth.

For the present purpose it is neither desirable nor necessary to deal with these debatable aspects of a question which from other points of view is full of interest.

It is held by some, although combated by others, that all the vestments of the Church had their origin in the regular dress of the citizens of Rome. Thus, Mr. R. A. S. Macalister, in his book on *Ecclesiastical Vestments* (1896), page 21, writes :—

We gather that, during the first centuries of the Christian Church, no vestments were definitely set apart for the exclusive use of the clergy who officiated at Divine service : that clergy and people wore the same style of vesture both in church and out, subject only to the accidental distinctions of quality and cleanliness.

The same writer points out that the symbolism which some writers have delighted to attach to the different vestments are as much accretions as are the jewels and the embroidery of the Middle Ages.

However this may be, one of the most striking things about ecclesiastical costume is the persistence with which certain definite types of vestment have been retained. The violent changes introduced into civil costumes, by which entirely new styles of garment. come instantly into fashion, are unknown in the formal official robes of the clergy. Here the changes of cut and material are gradual, and on the lines of continuous development and transition rather than of startling innovation.

Another point, to which allusion has already been made, is the richness of the materials and the wealth of ornament used in vestments of an ecclesiastical character.

The various garments of which ecclesiastical costume consists are well defined and easily recognizable when once understood, although the general ignorance on the subject is quite remarkable. For the purposes of definition it will be convenient to divide ecclesiastical costume into two broad classes, namely (1) eucharistic and (2) non-eucharistic.

1. EUCHARISTIC VESTMENTS

(i) AMICE. This garment, primarily perhaps a scarf, or a cloth for wrapping round anything, consisted of an oblong piece of linen with an ornamental edging or apparel affixed to one of its longer sides. There were also two strings attached to the two corners of the apparelled side, by means of which it was attached to the neck, the strings being passed under the arms, round the back, and tied on the breast. It was made to fall somewhat over the upper edge of the chasuble, with the result that it has often been mistaken for a collar of that vestment. As a matter of fact, the amice was the first of the eucharistic garments to be put on, whereas the chasuble was the last. The eucharistic amice must be clearly distinguished from the almuce or grey amice

Amice, from effigy of a priest, 1375

worn as a monastic and academical garment, which will be described in due course.

(ii) ALB.—The alb was a long close linen vestment, reaching from the neck to the knees, and furnished with fairly close-fitting sleeves. Apparels, or strips of orna-mental material, were sewn to the outer side of the sleeve close to the wrists, and to the middle of the front of the alb close to the feet. The chief part of the alb in the Middle Ages was composed of white material, and the apparels were in gold or coloured materials ; but in early times the whole garment was of ample size and ornamented with one or more scarlet strips in front.

Owing to the fact that the alb is usually nearly covered by the chasuble, so as to be visible only at the

wrists and near the feet, the graceful shape of this garment is rarely seen represented in sepulchral effigies. Fortunately, however, there are a few examples which, from one cause or another, enable one to see how the under garments worn at the celebration of the Mass were arranged. The monumental brass to a priest (name unknown), of about the year 1430, at Horsham Church, Sussex, is valuable in this way because, in addition to its being a beautifully executed figure, it shows a cope being worn over the amice, alb, crossed stole, and maniple. The cope is sufficiently open in front to allow one to see the whole arrangement quite well. Another figure, a statue in the chapel of the east transept at Lincoln Cathedral, represents a priest evidently vested for Mass, wearing amice, alb, and crossed stole, over which is a choir cope, open in front.

John West, chaplain, *circa* 1415 (Sudborough, Northants)

The best example for our purpose is unquestionably the effigy on the monumental brass to John West, Chaplain, of about the year 1415, at Sudborough, Northamptonshire. Here the figure is vested in all the

Mass vestments excepting only the chasuble, and no cope is worn. The result is that the precise arrangements of maniple and stole can be seen quite clearly.

The girdle, by which the alb was always tied closely round the waist, is in this case hidden by the falling over of the material of the alb above. The long ends of the stole are enclosed within the girdle in such a way as to keep them in their appropriate place, and also to preserve the crossed condition of the stole on the breast, an arrangement which was universally maintained in the case of priests wearing the eucharistic stole, but not in the case of bishops, the latter wearing it hanging down quite straight.

(iii) STOLE.—The chief peculiarity of this part of the eucharistic vestments has already been mentioned, consisting, as it does, in its being worn crossed on the breast, although the fact, owing to the chasuble being worn over it, is rarely to be detected. The stole may be defined as a long and fairly narrow band or scarf of embroidered silk or other rich material worn so as to pass from the back of the neck over the two shoulders, crossed on the breast, passed under the girdle of the alb, from that point both ends hanging down straight to a point about midway between the knee and the ankle of the wearer.

The origin of the stole is a matter upon which ecclesiological authorities are not in entire agreement, although it is pretty generally accepted that it represents the border of a Roman garment. Stoles belonging to the thirteenth and fourteenth centuries were often most beautifully worked in silk with sacred and heraldic devices and shields of arms. The famous Syon cope, now at the Victoria and Albert Museum, has an edging made apparently of a stole and maniple embroidered with arms set in small lozenge-shaped shields. Other extremely interesting examples of stole and maniple of the early part of the fourteenth century, or possibly the end of the thirteenth century, also embroidered with shields of arms, are in the possession of the Weld Family, at Leagram Hall, Lancashire, and they have been identified by Mr. Everard Green,[1] F.S.A., *Rouge Dragon*, as parts of the set of vestments which belonged to the Bridgettine nuns of Syon House, Isleworth, to which, of course, the Syon cope, just referred to, also belonged.

(iv) MANIPLE OR FANON.—This is believed to have been originally a narrow piece of linen used, as a modern handkerchief, for wiping the forehead, face, etc., but at an early period it was enriched with ornament. Fringed ends and embroidery in colours and gold were employed in the decoration of the fanon some time, according to some authorities, after the ninth century, but in the Bayeux Tapestry, it may be remarked, the representation of Archbishop Stigand shows the fanon plain and held in the left hand, which is open. By the fourteenth century it had become the practice to wear the fanon looped over the left forearm, purely as an ornamental part of a priest's vestments.

(v) CHASUBLE.—This was the outer garment of the eucharistic series, being placed over all those just

[1] See *Proceedings of the Society of Antiquaries of London*, XVII, 272-80.

described. It was worn only at the celebration of the Mass, and by the celebrant alone.

The chasuble is believed to have been originally of circular form with an aperture in the centre sufficiently large to allow of the head being passed through it. The materials employed in this important vestment, although originally simple, became in the course of time of the richest and most expensive kinds, and in order to permit the priest to perform his ministrations it soon became necessary to cut back the chasuble at the sides.

The old inventories give much information as to the materials of which chasubles were made in mediæval times. The following are a few samples chosen at random : " Red cloth of gold," " red velvet with Catherine wheels of gold," " red silk embroidered with falcons and leopards of gold," " white damask," and " purple satin." In shape the chasuble has varied from a round-ended oval to a pointed oval (or rather *vesica piscis* shape). Anciently it was the custom to make the back of the chasuble hang much lower down than the front, but the modern custom is to equalize the length of back and front. A fourteenth century chasuble preserved at Aix-la-Chapelle measures from the neck to the point in front 4 ft. 6 in. ; whilst from the neck to the point behind it measures 4 ft. 10 in.

There has been much discussion amongst antiquaries as to whether or not the chasuble and cope were originally the same vestment, or were derived from a common source. The question is considered in connection with the account of the cope.

Q

The chasuble has for so many centuries been regarded as the most characteristic of the sacerdotal
vestments that controversy and discussion have frequently and naturally been waged around it. Into
these points it is unnecessary and undesirable to enter
in these pages; but it may be well to point out that
the costliness of its materials and the elaborate character of its ornaments are due to the special significance which it has always had in the estimation of
Catholics.

The costliness of the material has already been
referred to; silk and cloth of gold seem to have
been freely employed, and the colours used were
doubtless generally in accordance with those proper
for the various seasons of the Church's year. It is
probable, however, that the richest and finest vestment was worn at the great festivals regardless of its
colour.

The chief ornament of the chasuble was the orphrey
(aurifrigium), a broad strip of elaborate embroidery
work applied to back and front of the vestment in
such a way as to hang in front from the neck in a
single band to the front point of the garment, and
at the back in the form of the letter Y, the two upper
limbs of which extended to each shoulder, whilst the
lower limb descended to the back point of the chasuble.

Of the vestments worn by assistants at Mass, the
dalmatic was the distinguishing garment of the deacon,
or gospeller, and the tunicle that of the sub-deacon.

(vi) DALMATIC.—There is reason to believe that in
the early ages of the Church the dalmatic was white

and identical with the alb, except that it was of some-what shorter proportions. In the Middle Ages the dalmatic was coloured to correspond with the chasuble.

The distinguishing feature of the dalmatic (which was so called from the fact that it had been worn in Dalmatia) was that it was slit up for a short distance on either side.

Some admirable mediæval examples of the dalmatic are depicted on the famous painted rood-screen at Randworth, Norfolk, including a figure of St. Stephen vested in an alb and green dalmatic, another of St. Laurence vested in alb and red dalmatic, another saint or bishop wearing the alb, a red dalmatic, chasuble, and purple gloves and mitre ; and another extra-ordinarily fine figure of a saint-archbishop, supposed to represent St. Thomas of Canterbury, wearing, in addition to the alb, amice, tunicle, dalmatic, and chasuble, the archiepiscopal pall. The letter T appears on the amice and on the orphrey of the chasuble.

The dalmatic was the special vestment of a deacon assisting at Mass.

The dalmatics of St. Stephen[1] and St. Laurence are

---

[1] It is noted that in the figure of St. Stephen, vested as a deacon, the right-hand side of the dalmatic is shown representing the slit as entirely edged with fringe. This is rather against the positive assertion of a recent writer that only the left-hand slit of a deacon's dalmatic was ornamented with fringe. The dalmatic of the bishop was, of course, fringed along the lower hems, the edges of the two slits, and the ends of both sleeves, but Mr. R. A. S. Macalister (*Ecclesiastical Vestments*, pp. 79–80) states that in the case of a deacon's dalmatic the left-hand slit, the lower hem, and the left-hand sleeve termination alone were fringed, the reason being simply that the fringe might be found inconvenient and in the way whilst the deacon was ministering at the altar.

enriched with an orphrey or apparel of great beauty decorated in bold conventional foliage and extending from the amice to the fringed hem of the dalmatic.

The whole series of pictures which are of the best fifteenth century period is remarkably fine both for artistic merit and as representing the costume of the time.

There is another pretty but quite simple figure of St. Laurence vested in a fringed dalmatic given on the brass to John Byrkhed, 1468, at Harrow, Middlesex.

(vii) TUNICLE. — This was a small variety of the dalmatic, and was worn specially as the distinguishing vestment of the sub-deacon assisting at the celebration of Mass, and also as one of the Mass vestments of the bishop.

Figure representing St. Laurence (Harrow, Middlesex). He is wearing only an alb and dalmatic

It may be remarked that in ancient accounts and inventories one usually finds the phrase "a pair of tunicles," which suggests that there was no other distinction formerly between dalmatic and tunicle except size.

Bishops and mitred abbots, in addition to the amice, alb, stole (not crossed in the case of bishops), fanon, and chasuble, wore tunicle, dalmatic, gloves, mitre, buskins, and sandals, also a ring on the second finger of the right hand, and a pastoral staff carried in the hand.

The following are brief particulars of the various episcopal garments :—

MITRE.—The distinctive head-covering of bishops and mitred abbots. Anciently the mitre was small and bore a reasonable proportion of the head of the wearer. There were three kinds of mitres, viz. (1) the *simplex*, of plain white linen, (2) the *aurifrigiata*, ornamented with gold orphreys, and (3) the *pretiosa*, enriched with gold and jewels in the most costly manner.

The twelfth century mitre of St. Thomas of Canterbury now preserved at Sens, and which has been well illustrated in one of the plates of Shaw's *Dresses and Decorations of the Middle Ages*, is a remarkably graceful example both in form and ornament. An elaborate form of fylfot has a prominent place in the decorative details of the horizontal and perpendicular bands. The mitre itself and the influœ or streamers which hang down from it are lined and edged with red material.

As time went on this simple tasteful mitre gave place to one of much larger and more ambitious character, and the great height of certain modern mitres is certainly not an improvement on the form once in use. The Limerick mitre (1418) is 13 inches high, whilst that of William of Wykeham (1403?), recently reconstructed, has been estimated at upwards of 17 inches.

There is an interesting specimen of a seventeenth century mitre of bowed form shown in the monumental brass of Samuel Harsnett, Archbishop of York (died in 1631), in Chigwell Church, Essex. The effigy is further remarkable on account of the square-cut beard which the prelate wears. It is what an old writer[1] describes as the " broad or cathedral beard."

[1] Randle Holme.

GLOVES.—Gloves were part of the habit of a bishop when vested for Mass and other solemn occasions. It

Episcopal gloves

is believed that the formal or official use of gloves did not commence until about the twelfth century, although, of course, they were in vogue as a protection from the weather at a much earlier date. The actual gloves of William of Wykeham are now preserved at New College, Oxford. Upon the back the letters "I H S" within the rays of the sun are worked. Episcopal gloves were sometimes jewelled on the back.

BUSKINS OR SABATYNS.—These were really stockings originally, fastened at the knee. In early times they were composed of linen, and afterwards of silk. Some interesting mediæval examples taken from the tomb of Hubert Walter, Archbishop of Canterbury, have been figured in *Vetusta Monumenta*, one of the publications of the Society of Antiquaries of London.

The buskins of Bishop William of Waynfleet, which are preserved at Magdalen College, Oxford, are figured in *Archæologia*, Vol. LX, p. 486.

SANDALS.—These were shoes, originally of open-work and afterwards, about the fourteenth century, furnished with strings. In addition to the representations of episcopal sandals on effigies and brasses, actual examples of those once belonging to Bishop William of Waynfleet and Archbishop Hubert Walter still exist.

PALL OR PALLIUM.—This was the distinctive ornament of an archbishop's ecclesiastical dress. In the Church of England this ornament, although retained in the arms of the sees of Canterbury and York, has not been used since the Reformation.

One of the best sources of information we have as to the vestments of a great ecclesiastical dignitary is the noble effigy of John of Sheppey, Bishop of Rochester, who died in 1360. The effigy is in his cathedral church at Rochester, and is specially remarkable for its good state of preservation and the completeness of its colouring—circumstances which are due to the fact that it, with several fragments of other carvings, had for many years been walled up in the choir, and covered with a large quantity of chalk.

The bishop, who had also filled the offices of Chancellor of the Realm and Treasurer, was a man of considerable importance in his day, and his effigy has evidently been carved and painted with great skill and care, and probably at no little expense. He is represented as completely vested in a bishop's Mass vestments, all of which are most thoroughly and minutely depicted. The head reposes on two highly ornamented pillows, but the various garments fall in graceful folds, as they might be expected to do in the case of a standing figure wearing garments of rich and costly materials.

NON-EUCHARISTIC VESTMENTS, INCLUDING PROCESSIONAL VESTMENTS

The processional vestments consist of the cassock, surplice, almuce, and cope, each of which requires a brief description. It may be added here, however, that the term processional does not imply that these vestments were worn only for processions, as they were used on many other occasions.

(i) CASSOCK.—This was one of the regular garments worn by men both lay and clerical during the Middle Ages. It was also worn by women, and may be described as a long loose coat or gown with tight sleeves, and fastened up the front. It can be traced from the eleventh century to the sixteenth century, when it was made much shorter, and became practically the short coat of recent times.

The cassock was really worn under the eucharistic vestments, but owing to the ample proportions of the alb it was not visible. In processional attire, however, the cassock was visible below the surplice.

Priest in cassock, about the year 1480 (Cirencester, Gloucestershire)

The chief purpose of the cassock was to keep the wearer warm, and its name in mediæval Latin, *pellicea*, was given because of its fur lining. The colour was generally black.

The form of the cassock, which in the fifteenth century formed the ordinary dress of the clergy and was also largely worn by the laity, is well shown in the figure of a priest here given, the date of which is about the year 1480.

(ii) SURPLICE.—This well-known ample garment of white linen was originally the alb, its greater size being probably due to the fact that it was intended to be worn over the fur-lined cassock. Indeed, its name, *superpellicea*, points to the same fact. The chief features which distinguish the surplice from other garments are its ample size, its plainness, and its very full and very wide sleeves.

Originally this garment, like the alb, was put on by being passed over the head, but the custom of wearing enormous wigs led to its being opened in front so that it might be donned without injury to the headpiece.

It is a curious fact that there has at times been strong antipathy to the surplice, especially amongst the strict Puritans.

The modern surplice is much less ample than the older form, and not nearly as graceful and becoming.

(iii) ROCHET.—This garment, like the surplice, was derived from the alb, now differing, however, from the surplice in having no sleeves.

(iv) CHIMERE.—This is a short coat which originally had no sleeves, but owing to some confusion as to the precise shape of ecclesiastical vestments, the tailors of the Stuart period transferred to the chimere the sleeves which originally and properly belonged to the rochet.

As now worn by the bishops the chimere is a black satin garment furnished with white lawn sleeves, drawn in and frilled at the wrists.

A learned paper on "The Black Chimere of Anglican Prelates : A Plea for its Retention and Proper Use " was read before the St. Paul's Ecclesiological Society in 1898, and is printed in the *Transactions* [1] of that society. The reader may be referred to this paper for further particulars on the subject.

(v) ALMUCE.—The almuce, like the cassock, was essentially a protective garment, intended for warmth and comfort rather than show or ritual purposes. It was both a hood and a cape, that is to say, it was adjustable so as to be used on the shoulders as a tippet, or as a hood if drawn over the head. The colour of the outside was usually black, but scarlet in the case of doctors of divinity. The lining was of fur, usually dark brown in colour, but for canons and doctors of divinity grey. The edge of the almuce was decorated with a number of tails of the animals from which the fur lining was made up. There are numerous effigies in brass which show this peculiarity.

Some valuable information in reference to the development of the form of the grey almuce is contained in Mr. W. H. St. John Hope's paper, "On Some Remarkable Ecclesiastical Figures in the Cathedral Church of Wells," published in *Archæologia*, Vol. LIV, pp. 81–6.

The two other effigies of canons at Wells [writes Mr. Hope] lie in the eastern aisle of the south transept.

[1] Vol. IV, pp. 181–220.

PORTRAIT OF DR. GEORGE ABBOT, ARCHBISHOP OF CANTERBURY
1611-1633

The southernmost represents William Byconyll, who died in 1448. He is shewn wearing the ordinary choir habit of cassock, surplice, grey amess and choir cope. The other figure is usually assigned to Henry Husee, who was dean of Wells from 1302 to 1305. The entire tomb is, however, clearly a century and a half later. The effigy is of alabaster, and represents a canon in cassock, surplice, grey amess and choir cope. Among the sculptured ornaments of the tomb are several small figures of canons holding books, also of alabaster. These have a peculiarity I have not noticed elsewhere. Each is represented in cassock, surplice, grey amess and choir cope, but the two pendent tails of the grey amess are held together on the breast by a cord which passes through them and hangs down with tasselled ends. This mode of fastening, which does not occur on the large effigy of the tomb, marks an interesting stage in the history of the grey amess.

The earliest effigies we have which represent this vestment are in the cathedral church of Hereford, where there are five figures in surplices and amesses. Three are by the same sculptor, and of early fourteenth-century date. One of the three, that erroneously assigned to Dean Borew, who died in 1461, but most probably representing John de Swimfeld, precentor in 1294 and 1311, is most carefully figured in Hollis's *Monumental Effigies*. The amess is here shewn like a short cope down to the elbows with long and pointed pendants in front and turned back round the neck like a loose, high-standing collar. The chief point to notice, however, is that the vestment is quite open in front and not joined on the breast, shewing that it was put on in the fashion of a woman's shawl.

The other two figures by the same carver shew a similar arrangement, but that assigned with some probability to dean John de Aquablanca, 1278–1320, has the amess clasped on the breast by a large morse.

This open form of amess is also seen apparently in another figure at Hereford, a priest in a cope from a cross brass, *circa* 1370. Several other brasses of this quarter of the century seem to shew the amess open down the front.

Passing on into the fifteenth century, when the little pendent tails became first common, the half effigy of William Tanner, master of Cobham College, who died in 1418, in his brass at Cobham, shews the grey amess clasped on the breast by a small brooch. Another brass at Cobham, that of Reginald de Cobham, who died in 1420, shews the amess open all down the front under his cope.

The Wells figures on the tomb under notice, and on the neighbouring tomb of William Byconyll, have the amice joined across. . . . An interesting survival of the old open shape may be seen at Hereford, where Dean Hervey, 1491–1500, has the amess secured by a large oblong brooch on the breast. The same effigy also shews the more ample development of the cope of the amess, which now began to be made longer behind and to completely cover the elbows. This form is admirably illustrated by the brass at Christ Church, Oxford, of James Courthope, canon of Christ Church and dean of Peterborough, who died in 1557.

(vi) Cope.—The probability is that the cope and chasuble were originally identical, or, at any rate, that they had a common origin. This relation is indicated by the Y-shaped cross on the back of the magnificent purple cope known as "casula St. Stephani," figured in Bock's *Klienodien Heil-Römischen Reiches Deutscher Nation*.

At a comparatively early period in the Middle Ages the cope became a very costly and elaborate vestment. It was generally made of cloth of gold or velvet, and was magnificently embroidered, jewelled, and enriched with precious metals. Some of the most effective and artistic of mediæval decorative efforts are to be found

Canon, 1413
(William Langeton, Canon of Exeter, in Exeter Cathedral)

upon garments of this kind. The cope is still worn when a cleric of sacerdotal rank ministers (i.e. assists) at Holy Communion; also by the celebrant at the Mass

of the Pre-sanctified on Good Friday, at solemn even-
song, and at funerals.

Probably the finest, certainly the most remarkable,
ancient cope of English manufacture is that known as
the "Syon Cope," in the Victoria and Albert Museum
at South Kensington.

It is of the latter part of the thirteenth century,
composed of linen in two and sometimes three thick-
nesses, embroidered all over with silver-gilt and silver
thread and coloured silks. The body of the cope is
covered with interlacing barbed quatrefoils outlined in
gold : the ground of these is embroidered with faded
red silk and the spaces between them with green silk,
worked so as to produce a chevron pattern on the surface. These quatrefoils are filled with scenes from the
life of Christ and the Virgin and figures of St. Michael
and the Apostles : the intervening spaces are occupied
by figures of angels, most of them six-winged and
standing upon wheels. The subjects are as follows,
taken from left to right :—In the upper row : St. Philip
with three loaves and book ; Christ Appearing to St.
Mary Magdalene in the Garden ; the Burial of the
Virgin, her body carried by the Apostles and attacked
by the Jews, whose hands are fixed to the bier, and her
soul borne by angels to heaven and dropping the
girdle for St. Thomas ; the Coronation of the Virgin,
enthroned beside Christ, who is blessing her ; the
Death of the Virgin, the Apostles surrounding her
and angels appearing from heaven ; the Incredulity of
St. Thomas, who thrusts his hand into the wound of
Christ ; St. Simon with short knotted club and book.

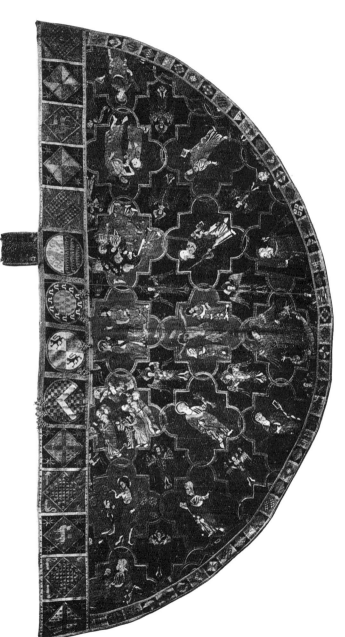

SYON COPE (LATE 13TH CENTURY)

(THE VICTORIA AND ALBERT MUSEUM)

In the second row : St. Bartholomew with knife and book; St. Peter with keys and book; Christ on the cross, His body worked entirely in silver thread, with the Virgin and St. John ; St. Paul with sword and book; St. Thomas with lance and book. In the third row : St. Andrew with saltire cross and book; St. Michael trampling on the dragon and thrusting a spear into his mouth ; St. James the Greater with staff and scrip and book. Portions of four other apostles with angels and lettering may be traced among the scraps with which the mutilated circumference of the cope has been patched ; at the upper edge, which has also been slightly mutilated, are two kneeling clerics, both holding scrolls inscribed DAVN PERS DE, with other lettering not at present decipherable. The figures are so placed as to be upright when the cope was worn, the centre of the back being occupied by the Coronation, the Crucifixion, and St. Michael. The faces, drapery, etc., are worked in very fine split-stitch with silk, the black and white parts of which have in some cases worn away. The broad orphrey, morse, and narrow semicircular edging (the latter apparently made out of a stole and maniple)[1] seem to have been added at a later date ; they are decorated with heraldic shields and emblems embroidered mainly in cross-stitch. On the orphrey are ten large lozenges, set alternately upon green and faded red grounds, arranged in groups of fives on each side of a central group of four large roundels on a green ground.

[1] See *Proceedings of the Society of Antiquaries*, XVII, 272.

The cope derives its name from the convent of Syon, at Isleworth, near London, founded, in 1414–15, by

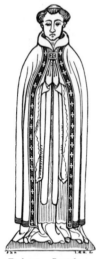

Robert London, priest, vested in cope, etc., 1416 (Chartham, Kent)

Henry V for the Bridgettine Nuns, into whose hands it came probably soon after their establishment. When the nuns left England in the early days of Queen Elizabeth they carried the cope with them on their wanderings through Flanders, France, and Portugal to Lisbon, whence they returned with it to England in 1830. After passing through the hands of the sixteenth earl of Shrewsbury, and Dr. Rock, it was acquired by the Museum from the Right Rev. Richard Brown in 1864.

The following official description of the Syon cope admirably explains the technical features of this remarkable piece of needlework :—

Cope, of canvas, entirely covered with embroidery of various classes ; the interlacing barbed quatrefoils are bordered with gold thread worked in close-lying short stitches, and three rows of green or red and yellow and white silks in chain stitch. The ground in the alternate quatrefoils is filled in with green and faded crimson silks worked in short stitches to form a close diaper of chevron silks pattern. On the inside of the embroidery hanks of loose thread have been laid, and are occasionally stitched over with the green and red silks passing through the intervening canvas, and so add substance to the embroidery. The quatrefoils enclose figures of our Lord, the Virgin Mary, and the Apostles ; with winged Cherubim or angels standing on wheels in the intervening spaces. The faces, hands, and coloured draperies are worked with fine coloured silks in small chain stitches. The gold embroidery is done in close-lying short stitches. The orphrey, morse, and hem are wrought with armorial bearings with coloured silks and gold and silver threads in small cross stitches, and are of later date (about fifty years).

The great elaboration of ornament expended upon copes, chasubles, and other Church vestments, the gold thread employed in the making and ornamentation of the materials, and the valuable stones, gems, gold clasps, etc., with which they were encrusted and adorned, rendered it necessary to make special provision for storing them in a place where they would be free from dust and out of the reach of thieves.

A remarkably interesting and perfect example of a mediæval vestry exists at the parish church of St. Peter Mancroft, Norwich, and fortunately not only the arrangements of the vestry but also a manuscript inventory of its contents taken during the first few years of the sixteenth century remains. The inventory is one of the British Museum manuscripts, and is marked MS. 871 in the Stowe Collection.[1]

This vestry was quite an important part of the church, and furnished with presses, coffers, etc., for the safe keeping of vestments, books, and other valuables. One press or set of aumbries contained four lockers, one above the other. In the topmost locker

---

[1] A paper on the subject was contributed in 1901 by Mr. W.. H. St. John Hope to the Norfolk and Norwich Archæological Society (*Norfolk Archæology*, Vol. XIV, pp. 153–240).

R

the plate was kept ; in the second were the grails ; in the third the processioners ; and in the lowest the grails.

Priest, 1530
(William Lawnder, in Northleach Church, Gloucester)

Special chests were made for the accommodation of copes. The cope-chest was a semicircular oaken box sufficiently large to allow the unfolded cope to lie inside. Examples of cope-chests remain at Gloucester Cathedral, Salisbury Cathedral, Wells Cathedral, Westminster Abbey, and York Minster.[1]

The use of semicircular chests for the accommodation of copes is interesting because it indicates persistence of form throughout a very long period.

In addition to the examples of actual English mediæval copes in our public museums and in private hands, the following churches possess specimens, according to Rev. G. E. Lee's *Glossary of Liturgical and Ecclesiastical Terms :*—Durham Cathedral 5, Ely Cathedral 1, Carlisle Cathedral 1, Salisbury Cathedral 2, Lichfield Cathedral 1, Westminster Abbey several ; whilst fragments remain at Bircham St. Mary's Church, Norfolk ; East Langdon, Kent ; and Romsey Abbey Church, Hampshire. Other old English copes and other vestments are preserved at the Roman Catholic College of St. Mary, Oscott, and at St. Chad's, Birmingham.

---

[1] See, for further particulars, *English Church Furniture.* By J. Charles Cox, LL.D., F.S.A., and Alfred Harvey, M.B., pp. 316–17.

CHAPTER XIII

MONASTIC, ACADEMIC, AND LEGAL COSTUME

IN the present chapter it is proposed to deal with three nearly related classes of costume, viz. monastic, academic, and legal.

MONASTIC COSTUME

The regular habit of the Benedictine monk comprised (1) *tunica*, or cassock, and (2) *cucullus*, or cowl. The cassock may be described as the body garment, or gown, whilst the cowl was a large loosely hanging garment with a hood attached to it and hanging sleeves.

The canons regular of St. Augustine wore a habit consisting of a fur-lined cassock, or pellicea, a white rochet concealing the furred cassock, and a plain but ample cloak with a small hood.

Examples of the dress worn by the Augustinian or Black Canons may be seen in the brasses at Dorchester (Oxfordshire), South Creak (Norfolk), and Over Wickendon (Buckinghamshire), in the incised slab at Warter Priory (Yorkshire), and in the stone effigies at Cartmel and Hexham.

Effigies of mediæval monks in England are rare, a circumstance (as the Rev. Herbert Haines pointed out in his *Manual of Monumental Brasses*) probably due to the rules of poverty by which their orders were bound. The accompanying illustration shows the habit of a fifteenth century monk at St. Albans Abbey.

We may next turn to the articles of female monastic attire, including abbesses, prioresses, nuns, and vowesses. For information on the last-named subject the reader may be referred to what has been said in reference to the costumes of widows (see pp. 179–182).

Examples of the dress of abbesses can be seen in the existing monuments, both in brass, at Denham, Buckinghamshire, and at Elstow, Bedfordshire. The former commemorates Dame Agnes Jordan, abbess of Syon, who died about the year 1544. The latter is to Dame Elizabeth Hervy, *circa* 1530.

A prioress is commemorated in the existing brass to Maria Gore at Nether Wallop, Hampshire, 1436, and there was formerly in the church of St. James, Clerkenwell, London, another monument to the memory of Isabella Sackville, the last prioress of the Benedictine Nunnery of Clerkenwell.

Robert Beauver, monk, of about the year 1470 (St. Albans Abbey)

Evidence as to the costume of nuns is to be found in several sepulchral monuments, including the following monumental brasses :—

Alianore de Bohun, Duchess of Gloucester, 1399, West-
    minster Abbey.

Eldest daughter of Sir Thomas and Lady Urswyk, 1470, at
    Dagenham, Essex.

Cicely, daughter of Thomas and Agnes Mountford, 1489,
    Hornby, Yorkshire.

Third daughter of Sir Thomas and Lady Barnardiston, 1503,
    Great Cotes, Lincolnshire.

Portion of effigy in
brass of a Prioress of
Kilburn. The wimple
is supported by a cord
which passes through
the veil over the fore-
head

Dame Alice Hamp-
ton, nun, about the
year 1510 (Michin-
hampton, Glouces-
tershire)

Dame Alice Hampton, probably a nun of Syon, *circa* 1510,
    Minchinhampton, Gloucestershire. She wears a rosary
    hanging from a girdle, and a ring on the third finger of
    the right hand.

Dame Joan Braham, 1519, Frenge, Norfolk.

Dame Joan Cook, 1529, St. Mary de Crypt, Gloucester.

Dame Susan Kyngeston, 1540, Shalstone, Buckinghamshire.

Margaret Dely, "a Syster professed yn Syon" (she was
    treasurer of Syon), 1561, Isleworth, Middlesex.

ACADEMIC COSTUME

There is a good deal of evidence on monumental brasses, effigies, and miniatures as to the forms of costume which in past ages were worn by persons of academical distinction. This phase of dress is closely associated with ecclesiastical costume. It resembles legal costume in having had its origin within the Church. The garb of schoolboys, as will be shown later on, is also intimately related to Church costume, because in former time the scholar was reckoned to be a minor ecclesiastic, or in minor ecclesiastical orders.

There are a good many monuments of one kind and another which represent persons having academical degrees and wearing the appropriate dress ; but it is not by any means clear in every case what the precise shape and material of those dresses are. The difficulty of depicting effigies on the flat surface of monumental brass plates is partly responsible for this, but in addition there is some doubt as to what the actual garments are.

It may be convenient at this point to consider the various academic garments represented, one by one, in order to make quite clear what the mediæval artist has not, in every case, depicted with complete perspicuity.

To begin with the head-dress : the pileus, or cap, the most distinctive garment of doctors, was of several shapes, but there are two main types, namely (1) the plain, close-fitting skull-cap, and (2) the round cap with a point in the centre and a general appearance of squareness in later examples indicating modification by use, resulting eventually in the regular square cap of modern times. This square appearance, it may be added, arises partly from use, and partly from the fact that there are four joins in the material. This species of cap is especially worn by doctors of divinity, S.T.P.'s, etc.

Doctor's cap, *circa* 1480

The hood, or caputium, was originally a regular mediæval form of head-dress, and was at one time worn by all the members of the universities, whether graduate or not. In process of time its use was restricted to the graduate members, and it then came to be reckoned a symbol or indication of degree. The hood, as worn by the undergraduate, is believed to have consisted of cloth without lining, whilst those worn by graduates were lined with fur or some other material. The distinction between the hood of the Master and the Bachelor was one of valuable material rather than form, the latter being, perhaps, unable to afford such a costly hood as the former. At an early period—the exact date is unknown—the hood was made to give way to a cap as a covering for the head, and the peak of the former was then allowed to fall down behind the back in the form of a species of liripipe. This was worn longer in the case of undergraduates in order to serve as a distinguishing mark differentiating them from graduates.

The tippet, or cape, was a garment composed of fur derived in all likelihood from the grey almuce—an ecclesiastical garment with which the black stole or scarf is closely associated. There is abundant evidence that the grey almuce was worn as a regular ecclesiastical vestment with the cope as one of the choir or processional vestments. The academical tippet was a dress of dignity and distinction.

There is an interesting representation of the dress of an Eton boy at Wyrardisbury, Buckinghamshire. The monument is in memory of John Stonor, an Eton scholar, who died in 1512. The gown, which is girded, is long and is cut somewhat closely to the figure, the sleeves moderately tight, and it is apparently lined with fur, fur appearing round the bottom and up the right side of the front. On the head is a curious cap with a small point in the centre, like a doctor's cap, with flaps covering the ears, and two short flaps, possibly parts of an academic hood, flowing behind the shoulders.

A garment which represents the origin of the modern academical hood is shown in the effigy of Dr. Richard Billingford (1442), who is depicted in the habit of a doctor, wearing, in addition to the doctor's cap and full gown, a large hood lined with fur.

A communication by Professor E. C. Clark on

Dr. Richard Billingford, Master of Corpus Christi College, 1442 (St. Benet's Church, Cambridge)

English Academical Costume was made to the Royal Archæological Institute[1] some years since, and it still remains the standard authority on a subject which every student of costume must admit is of the greatest interest, but also beset with many difficulties.

The following are the academic robes and garments which he describes:—

(1) TOGA or ROBA TALARIS, the simplest and most general form of university dress, was probably originally derived from the Benedictine habit. It was full and flowing, open in front with wide sleeves through which the arms passed their whole length. Subsequent modifications curtailed the sleeves for undergraduates (retaining the fuller form for mourning) and introduced distinctive marks for the various colleges. The modern Bachelor and Master of Arts gown is derived from this dress combined with other garments.

[1] *Archæological Journal*, Vol. L.

In certain colleges in Oxford it was directed to be sewn up from the wearer's middle to the ground. In Clare Hall, Cambridge, fellows are permitted to line it with fur.

(2) HOOD.—The hood (caputium) was originally the head covering in bad weather. It was afterwards dropped on the shoulders, and then assumed the form of a small cape. A large tippet is sometimes seen beneath this cape in representations of academical costume. The undergraduate's or scholar's hood was black, not lined, and to it a long liripipe or streamer was sewn at the back; the graduates' were furred or lined, and with a short liripipe. The various degrees were indicated by differences of lining; bachelors wore badger's fur or lamb's wool; licentiates and regents wore minever or some more expensive fur; non-regents wore silk. When the undergraduates abandoned hoods (before the sixteenth century—exact date uncertain) they became a distinctive mark of the attainment of a degree.

The LIRIPIPE was also called tipetum or cornetum. The latter may be the origin of the French cornette, a silk band formerly worn by French doctors of law, and a possible origin for the modern English scarf. The liripipe is also used to denote pendent false sleeves, and also the tails of long-pointed shoes. This, however, lies rather in the region of everyday costume. In 1507, at Oxford, we find typet or cornetum used to denote an alternative for the toga talaris allowed to Bachelors of Civil Law. This is clearly not the tail of a hood, but its exact significance is uncertain.

(3) MANTELLUM.—The origin and meaning of this word are alike uncertain. The use of mantelli or liripipia, commonly called typets, was prohibited to fellows and scholars of Magdalen College, Oxford, by a statute dated 1479, except *infirmitatis causa*. From this we may infer that the mantellus (also called mantella or mantellum) was something akin to the liripipe. In another notice (1239) they are coupled with cappae; certain riotous clerks had to march in penitential procession *sine cappis et mantellis*. Professor Clark infers from these passages and from other sources that the academical mantellum is not a hood but is worn either with, or in addition to, the hood, with the cope, or else instead of the cope or long tabard.

(4) CASSOCK.—This was at one time worn by all members of universities under their gowns. Doctors of divinity, doctors of law, cardinals, and canons wore scarlet. Certain days at present are called "Scarlet Days" in the English universities, on which doctors in all faculties wear scarlet.

(5) SURPLICE.—A dress of ministration, used in college chapels by non-ministrants, more as a matter of college discipline than as academical costume.

(6) ALMUCE.—Distinctive of masters and doctors, distinct by the hood. Another possible origin of the English hood.

(7) COPE.—There are two kinds of cope in use at the English universities—the *cappa manicata* or sleeved cope; and an uncomfortable contrivance called the *cappa clausa*, which was sewn all the way up, passed over the head when put on, and was not provided with

sleeves or other openings for the arms save a short longitudinal slit in front. The Archbishop of Canterbury prescribed this as a decent garb for archdeacons, deans, and prebendaries in 1222. Regents in arts, laws, and theology were permitted to lecture in a *cappa clausa*, or *pallium*, only. The *cappa manicata* was probably worn generally as being a sober and dignified dress ; it very rarely occurs in contemporary representations.

(8) The TABARD, or COLOBIUM, was a sleeveless gown closed in front; but ultimately it was slit up, the sleeves of the gown proper were transferred to it, and the use of the latter discontinued. All not yet bachelors were required by the statutes of Trinity Hall, Cambridge (1352), to wear long tabards, while Clare Hall, the adjoining foundation, required its master (head), master, and bachelor fellows to wear this and other robes, in 1359. King's Hall (1380) required every scholar to wear a *roba talaris*, and every bachelor a robe with tabard suited to his degree.

(9) UNIVERSITY HEAD-DRESS.—A skull-cap was early allowed to ecclesiastics to protect the tonsured head in cold weather, and, except the ordinary hood, this is the only head-dress recognized by the early university statutes. This *pileus*, however, soon assumed a pointed shape, and in this form was recognized as a part of the insignia of the doctorate ; doctors only are represented wearing it upon monuments. The central point developed afterwards into the modern tassel. Bachelors wore no official head-dress.

COSTUMES OF SCHOOLBOYS

The dark blue gown and yellow hosen of the scholars of Christ Hospital furnish one of the best examples of the survival to the present time of the ancient costume of boys.

Thomas Heron,
schoolboy, 1512
(Little Ilford,
Essex)

The ordinary costume of a schoolboy of the year 1512 is admirably portrayed in a monumental brass at Little Ilford, Essex. This is the brass to Thomas Heron, a schoolboy, who died at the age of fourteen. He wears a long gown with loose, open sleeves, and girded at the waist with a kind of strap from which hang a penner and ink-horn. The hair, which is indicated by straight perpendicular lines, is long, falling somewhat below the ears.

The dress of the Winchester scholars was a long gown, or toga talaris, with a hood, and according to the founder's provisions, a piece of cloth large enough to make a garment of this kind was given each Christmas to each scholar. The garment had, and still has, to be made up at the expense of the recipient. The scholars of Winchester were, by preference, chosen from the founder's kin, and for them the college supplied linen and woollen clothes, shoes, etc. The other scholars were provided only with the material for the gown; other garments had to be furnished by their friends. Fortunately an interesting representation of a Winchester scholar in the fifteenth century exists on a monumental brass in Headbourne Worthy Church, near Winchester. It commemorates John Kent, who was admitted to the school in 1431 and died at Headbourne Worthy, probably at the house of some relatives there, in 1434.

The long gown there shown is a quite simple garment falling from the shoulders to the level of the ankles, without any kind of girdle, and with fairly full sleeves drawn in smaller at the wrists This gown fits rather closely round the neck, and was evidently made to open in front, one button, a little below the chin, being visible. The dress is obviously that which was commonly worn about the middle of the fifteenth century. An incorrect drawing of the figure is given as the frontispiece, and is repeated on the cover of Mr. T. F. Kirby's *Winchester Scholars*, 1888.

The present-day dress of the Eton boys is too well known to need description. By the statutes of Henry VI (the founder) it was decreed that every scholar of Eton should receive yearly a gown and hood, twenty-four yards of cloth costing fifty shillings. This garment, it was provided, should not be sold, pledged, or given away, until it was three years old. Scholars and choristers were also supplied with clothing and bedding, but the total charge on this score should never exceed a hundred marks a year.[1]

At Wyrardisbury Church, Buckinghamshire, there is a very interesting effigy in brass of John Stonor,[2] who has often been referred to as an Eton school-

---

[1] *History of Eton College,* by Sir H. C. Maxwell-Lyte, 1899, p. 590.
[2] See page 249.

boy. As he died in the year 1512, the costume shown
would have been of great value as evidence for the
dress of Etonians in the early part of the sixteenth
century, but unfortunately there appears to be no
ground for the theory that Stonor was a scholar of
Eton, nor is there any evidence to show that he was
a boy at all, the curious cap and fur-lined garment
pointing rather to the effigy being that of a man.
Haines, nearly half a century ago, in his *Manual*,[1] referred to it as probably representing the dress of an
Eton scholar, and others have repeated the statement
without question. Druitt, in his valuable work, *Costume on Brasses*,[2] speaks of John Stonor positively as
" scholar of Eton." The dress, which will be found
described elsewhere in these pages, is very curious and
interesting, but there seems not the slightest reason to
suppose that it is at all like that ever worn by Eton
boys. What the Eton dress in the sixteenth century
was is not at all certain, but probably it resembled that
of the Winchester scholars of the day. The statutes
of Eton were largely founded on those of Winchester,
and the dress of the boys may very likely have been
influenced by Winchester in the same way, although
in their origin all the distinctive dresses of schools were
probably merely the ordinary dress of the boys of the
time when the schools were instituted.

LEGAL COSTUME

The legal profession was formerly closely associated
with religious orders, and in the tonsured crown and

[1] Page lxxxvi.   [2] Page 142.

the use of special robes on holy days we see this clearly indicated.

The robes, regularly worn by the judges and serjeants, according to the definition of Sir John Fortescue, consisted of (1) the coif, (2) a long robe (such as that once worn by priests) with a furred cape about the shoulders, and (3) a hood.

The coif, which is described as the "principal and chief insignment of habit wherewith Serjeants-at-law on their creation are decked," in its original state was intended to conceal the tonsure, because ecclesiastics were forbidden to practise as advocates in the civil courts. It was of white lawn or silk, forming a close-fitting head-covering, and resembling in form the characteristic cap of a Knight Templar. The coif was, indeed, the distinguishing mark of a serjeant-at-law. Like the berretta of the Church, and the doctor's academical cap, it denoted authority. That the purpose of the coif was to add dignity to the wearer is made very clear by the fact that the serjeants had the privilege of remaining covered even in the royal presence. The coif survived as a black silk patch with lawn edging in the middle of the wig, which was worn by serjeants and judges who were serjeants.

Other parts of judicial attire are the broad black silk scarf which hangs like a preacher's scarf, and which, probably, like it, was derived from the mediæval amice; the sach, corresponding with the ecclesiastical girdle; and the black cap, which is part of the full dress of judges, and is either carried in the hand or tucked into the sach on state occasions.

The mantle is worn by judges only at coronations, opening of Parliament, cathedral services, and on the first day of term.

The garment now known as a " gun-case " is the scarlet casting-hood, which some think was derived from a deacon's stole.

The robes worn anciently by the judges and serjeants are represented to-day by the scarlet and ermine garments still worn on the judicial Bench.

Formerly there was much variety of colour, although none of form, in the serjeants' robes. The accounts of the king's wardrobe show allowances to the judges of scarlet, minever, and green cloth "violet in grayn," etc., and the serjeants had to provide themselves with similar robes. At a call of serjeants in October, 1555, every serjeant subscribed for one robe of scarlet, one of violet, a third of brown-blue, a fourth of mustard and murrey, with tabards of cloth of the same colours.

Chief Justice of the King's Bench, 1439 (Sir John Juyn, St. Mary's Church, Bristol)

In early times the costumes of the judges and serjeants were fixed by quite definite regulations, but in agreement with the prevailing fashion of wearing parti-coloured garments in the middle of the fourteenth century, a good many variations of colour were introduced.

Some valuable details as to the costume worn by judges and other legal personages in the Courts of Chancery, King's Bench, Common Pleas, and Exchequer at Westminster in the fifteenth century, are contained in four illuminations believed to be of the time of King Henry VI, which were exhibited and described at a meeting of the Society of Antiquaries of London in 1860.[1]

The illuminations, which at that time were in the possession of Mr. Selby Lowndes, of Whaddon Hall, Buckinghamshire, appear to be all that was left of a manuscript abridgment of the law of earlier date than that of Fitzherbert.

In the picture of the Court of Chancery we have represented two judges in scarlet robes trimmed with white badger or lambskin, one of them being uncovered and tonsured and the other wearing a brown cap. On either side of the two seated judges sit two persons wearing mustard-coloured robes. These are the Masters in Chancery, and are represented as tonsured.

The registrars seated at a green-covered table have garments of blue and mustard-coloured materials. A clerk in mustard-coloured sleeved gown, with dark brown girdle, stands on the green table and reads a roll. At his side is an usher, clothed in parti-coloured gown of green and rayed blue, carrying a wand in the right hand.

[1] *Archæologia*, XXXIX, 357-72.

At the bar stand three serjeants wearing parti-coloured gowns of rayed blue, rayed green, buff, brown, etc., and also wearing capes over their shoulders and coifs on their heads.

In the picture of the Court of King's Bench there are five presiding judges, all attired in scarlet robes trimmed and lined with white material, probably fur, and all wearing coifs. Below the judges sit, all attired in parti-coloured dresses of blue (rayed) and buff, or murrey and green, the king's coroner and attorney and the masters of the court. Two ushers, clothed in murrey and rayed green and buff and rayed blue, stand on the green-covered table. Two coifed and parti-colour-attired serjeants stand one on either side of the prisoner. Other prisoners, awaiting trial, stand in the foreground under the charge of two tip-staffs or gaolers, one clothed in blue and the other in mustard-colour high cap and gown.

Seven crimson-robed judges are shown seated on the bench in the picture of the Court of Common Pleas. The prothonotaries and other officers of the court sit below, clothed in parti-coloured materials, in which one observes blue, green, and yellowish buff rayed with diagonal stripes of blue. The serjeants, wearing coifs, are also attired in parti-coloured gowns com-prising green, green rayed with white and red, blue, and blue rayed with pale green or white. The preva-lence of parti-coloured clothing and of rayed material in the costume of legal personages is remarkable.

The Court of Exchequer is presided over by a judge wearing scarlet robes and a scarlet hat. Two judges

SIR JOHN CLENCH, JUDGE OF THE QUEEN'S BENCH (DIED 1607)

robed and hatted in mustard colour sit on either side. Three serjeants stand at the table. They wear coifs and gowns and capes of parti-coloured and rayed materials of considerable variety.

A figure of one of the court officials in the foreground affords an extremely interesting example of a high-crowned hat of the period, which is thrown back over the left shoulder, where it is suspended by means of the long scarf or liripipe which was attached to the hat, and which, when the hat was on the head, hung down from it nearly to the feet.

The following are the regulations in force in 1635,[1] by which the use of the variously coloured robes was governed :—

The Judges in Term time are to sit at Westminster in the Courts, in their Black or Violet Gowns, whether they will ; and a hood of the same colour put over their heads, and their mantles over all ; the end of the hood hanging over behind ; wearing their Velvet Caps and Coyfes of Lawn, and cornered Caps.

The facing of their Gowns, Hoods, and Mantles is with changeable Taffata, which they must begin to wear upon Ascension Day, being the last Thursday in Easter Term ; and continue those Robes until the Feast of Simon and Jude ; And upon Simon and Jude's day, the Judges begin to wear their Robes faced with white furs of Minever ; and so continue that facing till Ascension Day again.

Upon all Holy days which fall in the Term, and are Hall days, the Judges sit in Scarlet faced with Taffata, when Taffata facing is to be worn ; and with Furs of Minever, when Furs of Minever are to be worn.

[1] Dugdale's *Originales Juridiciales*, pp. 101-2.

Upon the day when the Lord Mayor of London comes to Westminster to take his oath, that day the Judges come in Scarlet. And upon the fifth of November (being Gunpowder day), unless it be Sunday, the Judges go to Westminster Abbey in Scarlet to hear the Sermon; and after go to sit in Court. And the two Lords Chief Justices, and the Lord Chief Baron, have their collars of S S above their Mantles for those two days.

When the Judges go to Paul's to the Sermon, upon any Sunday in the Term time, or to any other public Church, they ought to go in Scarlet Gowns; the two Lords Chief Justices, and the Lord Chief Baron in their Velvet and Satin Tippets; and the other Judges in Taffata Tippets; and then the Scarlet Casting Hood is worn on the right side above the Tippets; and the Hood is to be pinned abroad towards the left shoulder. And if it be upon any grand days, as upon the Ascension Day, Midsummer Day, All Hallows Day, or Candlemass Day, then the two Lords Chief Justices, and the Lord Baron wear their collars of S S with long Scarlet Casting-Hoods and Velvet and Sattin Tippets.

At all times when the Judges go to the Council-Table, or to any Assembly of the Lords; in the Afternoons in Term time, they ought to go in their Robes of Violet, or Black, faced with Taffata, according as the time of wearing them doth require: and with Tippets and Scarlet Casting-Hoods, pinned near the left Shoulder, unless it be a Sunday, or Holy day, and then in Scarlet.

In the Circuit the Judges go to the Church upon Sundays, in the fore-Noon in Scarlet Gowns, Hoods and Mantles, and sit in their Caps. And in the after-Noons to the Church in Scarlet Gowns, Tippet and Scarlet Hoods, and sit in their cornered Caps.

And the first Morning at the reading of the Commissions, they sit in Scarlet Gowns, with Hoods and Mantles, and in their Coyfs and cornered Caps. And he that gives the

SIR MATTHEW HALE, LORD CHIEF JUSTICE OF ENGLAND 1671-1676

chardge, and delivers the Goal, doth, or ought for the most part, to continue all that Assizes the same Robes, Scarlet Gown, Hood and Mantle. But the other Judge who sits upon Nisi prius, doth commonly (if he will) sit only in his Scarlet Robe, with Tippet and Casting-Hood : or if it be cold he may sit in Gown, Hood and Mantle.

And where the Judges in Circuit go to dine with the Shireeve, or to a public Feast, then in Scarlet Gowns, Tippets, and Scarlet Hoods, or casting off their Mantle, they keep on their other Hood.

The Scarlet Casting-Hood is to be put above the Tippet, on the right side ; for Justice Walmesley, and Justice Warburton, and all the Judges before, did wear them in that manner ; and did declare that by wearing the Hood on the right side, and above the Tippet, was signified more temporal dignity ; and by the Tippet on the left side only, the Judges did resemble Priests. Whensoever the Judges, or any of them are appointed to attend the King's majesty, they go in Scarlet Gowns, Tippets, and Scarlet Casting-Hoods ; either to his own presence, or the Council Table.

The Judges and Serjeants when they ride Circuit, are to wear a Serjeant's Coat of good Broad-Cloth with Sleeves, and faced with Velvet.

They have used of late to face the sleeves of the Serjeant's Coat, thick with lace. And they are to have a Sumpter, and ought to ride with six men at the least.

Also the first Sunday of every Term and when the Judges and Serjeants dine at my Lord Mayor's, or the Shireeve's, they are to wear their Scarlets, and to sit at Pauls with their Caps at the Sermon.

When the Judges go to any Reader's Feast, they go upon the Sunday or Holy Day in Scarlet ; upon other days in Violet, with Scarlet Casting-Hoods, and the Serjeants go in Violet, with Scarlet Hoods.

When the Judges sit upon Nisi prius in Westminster, or

in London, they go in Violet Gowns, and Scarlet Casting-
Hoods and Tippets, upon Holy Days in Scarlet.

It may be added that much useful information about
the costume of judges, serjeants, etc., is contained in
the book entitled *The Order of the Coif*, by Alexander
Pulling, Serjeant-at-Law, and published in 1884.

JOHN, FIRST LORD SOMERS, LORD HIGH CHANCELLOR 1693-1701

CHAPTER XIV

CORONATION ROBES OF SOVEREIGNS AND PEERS AND PARLIAMENTARY ROBES

ROYAL CORONATION ROBES

THE vestments worn by English as well as many other sovereigns on the occasion of their coronation appear always to have been of a special character, not always alike in shape or style, but quite different from the costumes worn in Parliament and other great occasions.

The formal assumption of the crown and the other insignia of kingly authority forms one part only of the important ceremonies connected with what is known as a royal coronation. Anointing with holy oil and cream; the celebration of the Mass, or Holy Communion; the formal acknowledgment of the sovereign and universal acclamation of the fact; and the oath of allegiance solemnly taken by all ranks present, are the chief of the other parts of the ceremonial of coronation. What stands out quite prominently in all this is, not only the religious character of the proceedings, but also the fact that the sovereign himself, or herself as the case may be, assumes a position which belongs not wholly to the laity but is partly ecclesiastical. Indeed, in some European countries the emperor, on the occasion of his coronation, actually took part in the Mass, singing the Gospel as deacon.

The various garments, etc., which are worn as the special coronation robes have a remarkable affinity with the eucharistic vestments. They are as follows:

(1) COLOBIUM SINDONIS

This vestment, the first of the garments put on for the coronation ceremony, was so constructed, by being open up the sides and also by an opening on the left shoulder, that it could be put on and off easily. As an ecclesiastical, or rather, monastic dress, the colobium was the sleeveless dress of a monk, but from its position under the other garments as a coronation vestment, it resembles the alb rather than the tunic, as it has sometimes been called. The garment is composed of fine white linen, furnished with an edging of lace all round the margin, and a rich flounce of fine lace, nine inches in depth, hanging from the bottom.

Effigy of King Richard I (d. 1199) in Rouen Cathedral

(2) TUNICLE, OR DALMATIC

The dalmatic was worn sometimes by prelates as early as the fourth century. Originally this garment was proper to the deacons at Rome, and in time the privilege of wearing it was conceded to ministers of that order in other parts of the Church. Later on the same privilege was granted to abbots, and finally to kings and emperors, both at their coronation and when solemnly assisting at Mass. The garment worn by Queen Victoria, however, was considerably altered from its original form. It was opened up the front, and but for the unusually open sleeves, might be taken for a lady's jacket or mantle. It is composed of yellow cloth of gold, woven with green palm branches, from which issue roses, shamrock, and thistles. The lining is of rose-coloured silk.

(3) ARMILLA, OR STOLE

The armilla, or stole, used at the coronation of the late Queen Victoria, is a band of yellow cloth of gold three inches wide, and embroidered with Tudor roses, shamrock, thistles, and silver eagles with royal coronets between.

(4) IMPERIAL MANTLE

The imperial mantle worn at Queen Victoria's coronation was a magnificent vestment of yellow cloth of gold, woven with a golden branched pattern, and roses, thistles, and shamrocks. The lining is of rose-coloured silk, and the margins are decorated with gold fringe $2\frac{1}{2}$ inches deep. An oblong morse, attached to the upper part, provides the means of fastening the mantle. This is ornamented with an eagle between two palm branches in the centre, and the rose, shamrock, and thistle at the sides.

One is naturally struck by the apparent similarity of these coronation vestments with certain ecclesiastical garments. The colobium sindonis closely resembles the alb ; the tunicle, which is worn next, resembles the dalmatic, as we have seen ; and the armilla, worn over one shoulder and fastened under the opposite arm, reminds us of the stole worn by deacons. The imperial mantle, however, does not at first sight exhibit the same close relationship to Church vestments, but by some it has been supposed to resemble the back of a cut-down chasuble, and it is probable that this may be the correct solution.

We thus have the sovereign vested in the most essential of the eucharistic garments, and when we remember that Mass or Holy Communion has almost invariably been celebrated in connection with the coronation ceremony, the relation of the two sets of vestments becomes at once full of significance. By the consecration and coronation ceremony the sovereign was removed from the condition of the laity, and occupied a position little removed from that of the clergy. At the treasury of St. Peter's at Rome the imperial dalmatic of the German emperors is still preserved. It has been assigned to the twelfth century, and was worn by the German emperors when they were consecrated and crowned, and when they assisted the pope at the office of Mass. On those occasions the emperor discharged the functions of sub-deacon or deacon, and, vested with the dalmatic, chanted the Epistle and Gospel.

In England we have instances of the sovereign wearing eucharistic vestments. When the body of Edward I was exhumed at Westminster in the last century, it was found to be vested in dalmatic and stole, crossed in the priestly manner; whilst an effigy of Richard I shows that King vested in a cope-like mantle, dalmatic, and white sub-tunic, answering to the characteristic costumes of a bishop or priest, deacon, and sub-deacon.

The following details of the ceremony of coronation of Mary I and some subsequent sovereigns will doubtless be of interest :—

In her procession from the Tower of London to the royal palace at Westminster, Mary I is said to have been thus adorned : The Queen's Majesty richly apparelled with mantle and kirtle of cloth of gold, furred with minever and powdered ermines, having upon her head a circlet of gold, set with rich stones and pearls, in her Grace's litter richly garnished with white cloth of gold, with two trappers of white damask with cushions, and all things thereunto appertaining, according to the precedents. Then her Grace's footmen, in their rich coats, about her Grace on both sides. Then the canopy of rich cloth of gold, furnished according to precedents, borne by the knights, with certain other knights appointed for assistants to them.

On the coronation day, Mary, in her Parliament robes of crimson velvet, under a rich canopy of baude-

kin, borne by the barons of the Cinque Ports, proceeded to Westminster Abbey. After a sermon had
been preached, prayers said, and the oath administered,
the Queen was newly apparelled in crimson velvet, viz.
a robe containing a mantle with a train, a kirtle furred
with minever, a surcoat, a riband of Venice gold, the
mantle of crimson velvet powdered with ermines, with
buttons and tassels of silk of gold for the same, in
which robes she received her ointments and also the
imperial crown.

During the ceremony of the anointing with the holy
oil and cream a pall was held over the Queen by four
Knights of the Garter. Then after her injunction the
Bishop of Winchester dried every place of the same
with cotton or linen cloth, "and after Mrs. Walgrave
did lace again her Highness's apparel, putting on her
hands a pair of linen gloves." After this the Queen
again put on her rich robe of crimson velvet, and then
the swords, sceptres, crown, and other regalia.

When Queen Mary was completely invested with
the coronation robes and the regalia, she is said to
have had "a pair of sabatons on her feet, covered
with crimson cloth of gold, lined with crimson satin,
garnished with riband of Venice gold."

Mass was next celebrated, and then the coronation
robes were taken off, and other royal apparel given to
her by the Great Chamberlain, consisting of a robe of
purple velvet, with the kirtle and surcoat open, and a
mantle with a train furred with minever and powdered
ermine, and a mantle lace of silk and gold, with buttons
and tassels of the same, and riband of Venice gold, the

crown set upon her head, and a goodly canopy being borne over her by the barons of the Cinque Ports.

The coronation vestments used by Queen Elizabeth were probably identical in character with those which had been worn by Mary. A contemporary account of the ceremony is preserved in a manuscript in the Ashmole collection at Oxford, and, although it is simply the record of what a spectator saw and heard, without the assistance of any official information, there is a good deal of useful information in it.

After Mass had been sung by the bishop, a carpet was spread before the high altar, and cushions of gold were placed upon it. The Queen, being newly apparelled (doubtless in the coronation robes proper to the solemn occasion), now came before the altar and leaned upon the cushions, and over her was spread a silken cloth (canopy), and then the bishop anointed her Grace. This done, she changed her apparel and returned and sat in her chair. Then a sword with a girdle was put upon her, the belt going over one shoulder and under the other, so that the sword hung at her side, and then two garters were put upon her hands, and the bishop put the crown upon her head, and the trumpets sounded. Then the bishop put a ring upon her finger and delivered the sceptre into her hand, and after that put another crown upon her head ; the trumpets again sounded.

The coronation of James I was similar in many of the details to that of Elizabeth. The principal variations in the coronation of Charles I were the presenting the King with St. Edward's Staff at the door of Westminster Abbey, who walked with it up to the throne, and the girding of his Majesty with three swords instead of one.

The coronation of Charles II approached more nearly the present form, and that of James II differed from his brother's principally in the omission of the Communion service.

Immediately the crown is placed on the head of the sovereign at the coronation ceremony, the peers and peeresses place upon their own heads the coronets proper to their rank, and which until this moment in the ceremony they have been holding in the hand.

PEERS' AND PEERESSES' CORONATION ROBES

The costume worn by peers on the occasion of the coronation of the sovereign are of considerable antiquity. The following official order given 1st October, 1901, and published in the *London Gazette* of 29th October, 1901, contains useful information on the subject :—

"The Earl Marshal's Order concerning the Robes, Coronets, etc., which are to be worn by the Peers at the Coronation of Their Most Sacred Majesties King Edward the Seventh and Queen Alexandra.

"These are to give notice to all Peers who attend at the Coronation of Their Majesties, that the robe or mantle of the Peers be of crimson velvet, edged with miniver, the cape furred with miniver pure, and powdered with bars or rows of ermine (i.e. narrow pieces of black fur), according to their degree, viz. :—

> Barons, two rows.
> Viscounts, two rows and a half.
> Earls, three rows.
> Marquesses, three rows and a half.
> Dukes, four rows.

"The said mantles or robes to be worn over full Court dress, uniform, or regimentals.

"The coronets to be of silver gilt; the caps of crimson velvet turned up with ermine, with a gold tassel on the top; and no jewels or precious stones are to be set or used in the coronets, or counterfeit pearls instead of silver balls.

"The coronet of a Baron to have, on the circle or rim, six silver balls at equal distances.

"The coronet of a Viscount to have, on the circle, sixteen silver balls.

"The coronet of an Earl to have, on the circle, eight silver balls, raised upon points, with gold strawberry leaves between the points.

"The coronet of a Marquess to have, on the circle, four gold strawberry leaves and four silver balls alternately, the latter a little raised on points above the rim.

"The coronet of a Duke to have, on the circle, eight gold strawberry leaves.

"By His Majesty's Command

"NORFOLK

"Earl Marshal"

The following regulations respecting the robes of peeresses were issued at the same time :—

"These are to give notice to all Peeresses who attend at the Coronation of Their Majesties, that the robes or mantles appertaining to their respective ranks are to be worn over the usual full Court dress.

"That the robe or mantle of a Baroness be of crimson velvet, the cape thereof to be furred with miniver pure, and powdered with two bars or rows of ermine (i.e. narrow pieces of black fur); the said mantle to be edged round with miniver pure two inches in breadth, and the train to be three feet on the ground; the coronet to be according to her degree, viz. a rim or circle with six pearls (represented by silver balls) upon the same, not raised upon points.

T

" That the robe or mantle of a Viscountess be like that of a Baroness, only the cape powdered with two rows and a half of ermine, the edging of the mantle two inches as before, and the train a yard and a quarter ; the coronet to be according to her degree, viz. a rim or circle with pearls (represented by silver balls) thereon, sixteen in number, and not raised upon points.

" That the robe or mantle of a Countess be as before, only the cape powdered with three rows of ermine, the edging three inches in breadth, and the train a yard and a half ; the coronet to be composed of eight pearls (represented by silver balls) raised upon points or rays, with small strawberry leaves between above the rim.

" That the robe or mantle of a Marchioness be as before, only the cape powdered with three rows and a half of ermine, the edging four inches in breadth, the train a yard and three-quarters ; the coronet to be composed of four strawberry leaves and four pearls (represented by silver balls) raised upon points of the same height as the leaves, alternately, above the rim.

" That the robe or mantle of a Duchess be as before, only the cape powdered with four rows of ermine, the edging five inches broad, the train two yards ; the coronet to be composed of eight strawberry leaves, all of equal height, above the rim.

" And that the caps of all the said coronets be of crimson velvet, turned up with ermine, with a tassel of gold on the top.

" By His Majesty's Command

" NORFOLK

" Earl Marshall"

These directions, although issued in the twentieth century, are equally true in reference to the robes and coronets worn by peers and peeresses at coronations

THOMAS PELHAM HOLLES, DUKE OF NEWCASTLE (IN THE ROBES OF
THE ORDER OF THE GARTER), PRIME MINISTER 1757-1760

for many years past, certainly as long ago as the
early part of the eighteenth century. The various
" rows of ermine " referred to are lines of black dots on
the white ermine cape. When two and a half rows (as
in the case of a viscount) are mentioned, the method of
representing them was by means of two horizontal
bands or rows of dots extending completely round the
cape of fur, and, on the right side, a third band
extending from the front to the back only. In the
case of an earl, three complete rows of dots extending
horizontally round the cape are worn.

The full coronation robes of peers consist of surcoat
edged with ermine, robe lined and edged with ermine,
an ermine cape (with collar) marked with black dots to
denote degree, and coronet, full court dress, or naval
or military uniform, being worn beneath.

The following is a brief account of the splendid
dress worn by the Gentlemen of the Privy Chamber on
the occasion of the coronation of George IV.

A Garter blue satin Jacket, slashed with bright
scarlet satin, and edged with gold spangled gymp.
Garter blue satin Rosette on the right shoulder, with
long pendent bows and ends, and edged with gold
spangled gymp.

A pair of Garter blue satin Trunks, slashed with
bright scarlet satin, and edged with gold spangled
gymp.

A Garter blue satin Surcoat, lined with bright scarlet
silk, and hanging sleeves.

A pair of Garter blue silk long Hose, affixed to
elastic Drawers.

A white hooked muslin Ruff.

Knee-bands and Rosettes of Garter blue satin, edged with gold spangled gymp.

White kid Shoes with blue heels, Rosettes with gold spangled gymp, of Garter blue satin.

Chapeau of Genoa black velvet, with scarlet and black Plume.

A pair of white kid Gloves.

Sword, with gilt hilt, and Garter blue satin Scabbard.

Blue satin Sword-belt, with large gilt Centre Buckle, and small gilt Buckle below.

PARLIAMENTARY ROBES

The effigies of King Richard II and his queen, in Westminster Abbey, are shown as wearing Parliament robes.

The parliamentary robes of peers differ from this arrangement considerably. The robes are of scarlet cloth (not crimson velvet, as in the case of the coronation robes), and the different degrees of baron, viscount, earl, etc., are marked by horizontal bands of ermine alternating with gold lace bands on the robe itself.

This type of robes is well shown in the portrait of Thomas Egerton, Viscount Brackley, who was Lord Chancellor of England from 1596 to 1617. (See frontispiece.)

EFFIGIES OF KING RICHARD II, AND HIS QUEEN, ANNE OF BOHEMIA.
WESTMINSTER ABBEY (IN PARLIAMENT ROBES)

CHAPTER XV

ROBES OF THE ORDERS OF CHIVALRY, OFFICIAL HERALDIC COSTUME, CIVIC ROBES, ETC.

ORDER OF THE GARTER

THE habits worn by members of the Order of the Garter consist of :—

      (1) The garter ;
      (2) The mantle ;
      (3) The surcoat ;
      (4) The hood.

The garter was made of blue cloth or silk embroidered with gold, with the motto "Hony soit qui mal y pense" worked in gold, and the buckles, bars, and pendants of silver gilt. Some of the ancient accounts describe the garter as made of blue satin, tartarin, or taffeta, lined with buckram and card of like colour and embroidered with Cyprus and Soldat gold and with silks of various colours.

The mantle resembled, in fashion, the pallium or toga of the Romans. It was without sleeves, covered the whole body, and reached down to the ankles. In place of the buckles or clasp, by which the toga had been fastened on the right shoulder, the mantle was drawn together at the collar by a pair of long strings, called cordons, robe-strings, or laces, woven of blue silk, and terminating in tassels of silk and gold thread. The material of the mantle was woollen cloth; the colour blue; the lining was of scarlet cloth. In the case of the sovereign, however, the mantle was lined with ermine, had a longer train than the rest, and was powdered all over with small garters embroidered with silk and gold.

The surcoat, or supertunica, was worn next under the mantle and over the vest. It was narrower and shorter than the mantle, and fastened to the body by a girdle. Like the mantle, the surcoat was formerly made of woollen cloth. The colour of this garment was changed every year, blue, scarlet, sanguine in grain, white, and black, being employed at different times. Sometimes the surcoat was embroidered with the arms of the knight who wore it. The surcoat of the companions was lined with miniver, whilst that of the sovereign was purpled with ermine.

The hood was in use in the time of Edward III, and was originally intended to serve as a defensive covering for the head. It was made of the same material as the surcoat.

The cap, afterwards introduced, did not supersede the hood, which was retained and worn hanging down the back in the manner of a pilgrim's hat.

A monumental brass in Magdalen College, Oxford, commemorating Arthur Cole, Canon of Windsor, who died in 1558, has an effigy of the canon wearing cassock, almuce nebulé at the edges, and a mantle

ROBES OF THE MOST NOBLE ORDER OF THE GARTER

of the Garter with St. George's Cross on the right shoulder.

There are two other examples of the mantle of the Garter in monumental brasses, namely, that to Roger Parkers, North Stoke, Oxfordshire, *circa* 1370; and Roger Lupton, LL.D., Provost of Eton and Canon of Windsor, in Eton College Chapel, 1540.

A gold collar composed of pieces in the form of the Garter and weighing thirty ounces troy-weight was ordered by the statutes of 1522 to be worn round the neck on certain specified occasions.

It may be added here that many of the pictures and statues of English sovereigns which are often popularly supposed to represent the coronation vestments really depict the mantle, surcoat, etc., of the Order of the Garter.

ORDER OF THE THISTLE

The habits of the Order of the Thistle comprise :—

Under-habit consisting of doublet and trunk-hose of cloth of silver; breeches and sleeves garnished or ornamented with silver and green ribands; stockings of pearl-coloured silk; shoes of white leather; and garters and shoe-strings of green and silver.

Surcoat and *hood* of rich purple or garter blue velvet, lined with white taffeta, girded with a sword-belt of purple velvet trimmed with gold lace.

Mantle, or *robe*, of rich green velvet, lined with white taffeta.

Cap of black velvet, faced up with a border of the same, a little divided before, wide and loose in the crown, and having a large plume of white feathers, with a black egret or heron's top in the middle of it.

ORDER OF THE BATH

The habits of the Order of the Bath comprise under-habit, surcoat, mantle, and cap.

These vestments may be thus briefly described :—

Under-habit.—This consists of a doublet of white satin, white hose, boots of white kid leather, gilt spurs with white leathers, white girdle without ornaments, white gloves, sword with gilded pommel and cross-bar, and white scabbard with gilt furniture.

Surcoat is of crimson satin, lined with white ducape silk.

Mantle.—This is the most ancient part of the habit of the Order, and closely resembles the original pattern. It is made of rich crimson satin, lined with white ducape silk, with the star embroidered on the left side. On the left shoulder is placed the lace of white silk anciently worn by the knights. The mantle is fastened at the neck by a long cordon of white silk, having at each end a crimson silk tassel, netted and fringed with gold.

Cap.—This was formerly of white satin, adorned with a standing plume of white ostrich feathers, but at the coronation of George IV the colour of the cap was changed to black.

Blue mantles were sometimes worn until the year 1725, since which date the colour has uniformly been crimson.

HERALD, 1561

HERALD, 1576

ORDER OF ST. PATRICK

The habits of this Order comprise :—

Under-habit, doublet, and trunk-hose of white satin, trimmed with silver plate lace ; stockings of white silk, with crimson knee rosettes ; boots of white kid leather, turned up with sky-blue, with red heels, and a bow of crimson riband on the instep.

Surcoat of sky-blue satin, lined with white silk.

Mantle of rich sky-blue satin, lined with white ducape silk. It has a hood of blue satin, also lined with white silk.

Hat.—This was originally round in form, covered with white satin, and lined with blue ; but in 1821 it was commanded by George IV that a black velvet hat, without band, should be worn instead.

ORDER OF ST. MICHAEL AND ST. GEORGE

The habit comprises :—

Mantle, or *robe,* of Saxon blue satin, lined with scarlet silk, and

Cap made of blue satin, lined with scarlet, turned up in front, with a representation of the star of the Order embroidered upon it, the cap being surmounted by three white ostrich feathers, with one large black ostrich feather in the middle.

OFFICIAL HERALDIC COSTUME

The official habit of a herald is a tabard—a garment which has been described as "a jacquet or sleeveless coat worn in time past by noblemen in the warres, but now only by heraults, and is called their coat of armes in servyse " (*Spight's Glossary*, 1597).

Whatever may have been the reason which induced heralds to adopt this distinctive costume, there is no doubt that they have long worn it. The tabard was a familiar article of apparel in the time of Richard II, and it was adopted as the sign of a well-known inn in Southwark at that period, but it is believed that in this instance a tabard of the kind worn by poor plough-men, a species of rough working gown, was typified.

Planché is unable to find evidence of a military tabard before the reign of Henry VI. Heralds do not seem to have come into existence earlier than the fifteenth century.

Henry VI is the first English sovereign who is represented on his great seal in a tabard, embroidered with the arms of France and England quarterly.

The duties of heralds in former times were manifold, including the following :—(1) To make royal and state proclamations; (2) to bear ceremonial messages between princes and sovereign powers; (3) to make proclamations in the tourney; (4) to convey challenges; (5) to marshal combatants; (6) to arrange public processions, funerals, and other state ceremonials; (7) to regulate the use of armorial bearings; (8) to settle questions of precedence, and (9) to keep official records of pedigrees, etc.

The tabard, it may be supposed, was intended to indicate that they represented the royal authority, as the garment was already one of the regal robes.

In addition to the tabard emblazoned with the royal

arms, the herald wears a collar of SS. The king-at-arms wears, moreover, a crown formed of a golden circlet, from which rise sixteen oak-leaves. On the circlet itself are the words :—

"MISERERE MEI DEUS SECUNDUM MAGNAM
MISERICORDIAM TUAM."

(Have mercy on me, O God, according to
Thy great loving-kindness.)

CIVIC ROBES

The robes worn by the mayors and aldermen of corporate towns are of considerable antiquity, although, as the late Llewellyn Jewett has pointed out,[1] there appears to be no available evidence on the subject earlier than the fifteenth century. In the year 1463 civic personages in England were expressly excepted, in the ordinance against excessive apparel, from the disability to wear garments trimmed with fur. Similar privileges were given in subsequent sumptuary laws.

The mayor and aldermen of London, on festivals and state occasions, wore, as early as the year 1415, scarlet gowns, but on other occasions violet or black gowns were worn.

During the same century Hull and Nottingham followed this rule. About the end of the fifteenth century the Mayor of Bristol wore a "Skarlat cloke, furred, with his blak a lyre hode, or tepet of blak felmet."

---

[1] *Corporation Plate,* by Jewett and Hope, I, lxxxvii. We are indebted to this work for most of the facts here given.

At York, scarlet, murrey, crimson, violet, and blue gowns were worn by the aldermen in 1482 and 1483. The corporation of London wore scarlet in 1483.

In the sixteenth century the wearing of scarlet gowns on festival days was the regular custom in all the more important towns. In 1530 the ex-bailiffs and ex-chamberlains of Oxford wore crimson gowns wherewith to attend the mayor on Ascension Day, and every common councillor was to have a murrey gown. The habit of the Mayor of Oxford in 1554 was ordered to be, as formerly, "a scarlett gowne, a scarlett cloke, and a tippett of velvet"; and in 1577 the mayor, aldermen, and associates and ex-bailiffs were directed to wear scarlet gowns, the chamberlains crimson, and the councillors murrey at all solemn meetings and feasts.

In 1541–2 the bailiffs and ex-bailiffs of Great Yarmouth were enjoined to wear on all principal feasts "gowns of scarlet furred with foynes, tippets, and doublets of velvet, after the ancient and honourable custom of the town."

At Wells, in 1547, the aldermen (the local name was masters) wore scarlet on the seven principal feasts. In 1585 they were directed to have their gowns faced with foynes, the mayor and the master who was justice of the peace being further distinguished by black and velvet tippets respectively.

At the period of the Commonwealth civic gowns were in some places discontinued, and not resumed until after the Restoration. But in some towns the old state of things was continued.

The aldermen of Kendal wore violet gowns "for

Sheriff of the City of York, 1642

best," and black for ordinary occasions.   At Faversham the Jurats wore black.   At Newbury and Preston the mayor and aldermen wore blue gowns.

The sheriffs of London and York wore scarlet ; those of Chester, Lincoln, and Norwich, however, wore purple.

The formal head-dresses of civic personages was in the south of England those known as " beavers."   At Carlisle, in 1634, the mayor and aldermen wore blue bonnets.

The orders which made it necessary for mayors to wear scarlet also required their wives to wear gowns of the same colour, fines being imposed in cases of non-compliance.   These rules were in force chiefly during the sixteenth century.

When a sovereign visited a town the mayor and aldermen put on their best array, and were accompanied by an imposing body of the commonalty wearing gowns and hoods, usually of the city's livery, such as red and white at London, and green and red at Coventry.

The liveries of serjeants, criers, beadles, constables, and other servants of the corporations were provided for by yearly allowances.   Cloth of ray, or striped cloth, was the usual material employed for their garments.

CITY LIVERY COMPANIES' GOWNS, ETC.

The liveries of the different London Companies are not traceable, according to William Herbert,[1] before

[1] *History of the Twelve Great Livery Companies of London,* I, 59.

the reign of Edward I. In Strype's edition of Stow mention is made of a procession of the citizens in 1299, on Edward I's marriage, at Canterbury, with his second queen, Margaret, when the fraternities rode, to the number of six hundred, "in one livery of red and white with the connuzances of their mysteries embroidered on their sleeves." At the marriage of Henry III the citizens of London wore a kind of uniform costume, which, from the fact that there were no distinguishing marks between different bodies, can hardly be called livery in the true sense.

The Grocers' Company, at their first meeting in 1345, prescribed the wearing of a livery. The Company's ordinances in 1348 describe the common habit as an under and an upper garment, called a "coat and surcote"; the cloak, or gown, and the hood, being reserved for ceremonials, and completing what was termed the full suit. There seems also to have been an undress, or part dress, called "the hooding," perhaps allowed to freemen, who were not esteemed "full brothers," like the livery.

Great variations of colour were worn by the Companies until the matter was regulated and settled, about the beginning of the seventeenth century : the fashion or form of the garments had long been pretty much as it is at the present time.

In 1414 the Grocers wore scarlet and green ; in 1418 scarlet and black. At the beginning of the reign of Henry VI the same company wore murrey (that is, dark red) and plunket (a kind of blue).

Various other colours, it is recorded, were worn,

including "sanguine," "cloth of blood-colour," "grene cloth," "cloth parted with rayes" (or striped cloth).

In the well-known picture of Paul's Cross painted on a wooden diptych in the possession of the Society of Antiquaries of London the citizens are shown sitting to hear the sermon all wearing a livery of black edged with red. This is worn probably because the King and his court, the judges and the Lord Mayor, and other civic dignitaries are present.

In the reign of James I the livery dress had reached practically the same form as that now worn, the chief points of difference consisting in the caps and hoods and long furred lappet pendent from the gown-sleeves which were worn in the seventeenth century. The gowns were, as now, of black material, and trimmed with " budge " or " foins."

U

INDEX

PRINTED BY
WILLIAM BRENDON AND SON, LTD.
PLYMOUTH